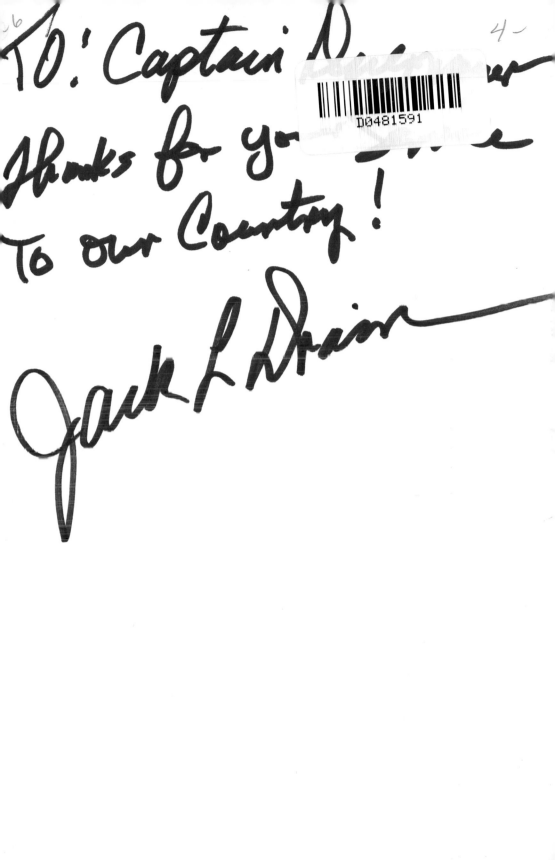

To: Captain D[...]
Thanks for y[...]
To our Country!

Jack L Drain

Praise for *Life On a Short Fuse*

If you really want to know what happened in Vietnam, don't ask the reporters or even authors with something to gain by selling their stories to a mass-marketed media that controls much of the content of what we read. Instead, read Jack Drain's *Life on a Short Fuse*.

Here you will understand why so many are the "walking wasted"— proud young warriors who suffered through a confusing war and even worse homecoming. A Christian, both then and now, the author recounts his experiences and questions while giving us the straight-forward facts about the philosophies, targets, ordnance, planes, and men he worked with through a fascinating career of service.

It has taken a period of nearly forty years for the true stories of Vietnam to come to light. Drain's chronicles add the perspective of a decorated career pilot, family man, and man of faith. Proud of his service, and yet able to question war, this will cause the reader to see Vietnam and today's wars in a new light. Only by reading and taking to heart these lessons will we learn about the atrocities of war and the brave warriors who fight them.

Read *Life on a Short Fuse* whether you're a veteran or not. Read it whether you're a Christian or not. Read it if you want the truth from a man who was there and still wrestles with it today. Whatever your motivation, this book should be read more than once and shared with your friends.

Patrick J. McLaughlin, CDR, USN
Iraq War Veteran and Former Chaplain at Camp David
Author of *No Atheists in Foxholes: Prayers and Reflections from the Front*

Jack Drain has written an accurate and thought-provoking book that depicts the life of a career AF officer in time of peace and war. We shared pilot training, the Korean War, and came back together for Vietnam—a war fought against an enemy with no respect for human life or code of conduct.

I well remember our fight against using a bomb fuse we knew to be faulty, of the stubborn resistance and leadership of (then) Col. Boots Blesse, and the ultimate rejection of the devise. Jack vividly and accurately describes this period and the terrible consequences of technology failure along with the loss of lives and the imprisonment and torture of our squadron mates. It is a tough and honest story of a turbulent time in America's history written by a humble man of God for the veteran and all those who need a better understanding of that period.

Major General Warren C. Moore, USAF, (ret.)
Major-Lt. Col., Danang, RVN, August 1967–June 1968

Now and then a book comes along that truly *needs* to have been written. Such a book is *Life on a Short Fuse*. Lt. Col. Jack Drain is a genuine American patriot, and he has provided us with a glimpse into the horrors of war as one who has experienced it firsthand. Yet he has done so with a goal toward the ultimate healing of hurts too long unattended and overlooked. Those who served our nation honorably in the Vietnam War, many of whom gave their all, deserve to have this story told. Although it is for them, it is also for us who remain to ensure they are never forgotten. The author is a man of faith who has dared to challenge us to look into the past and to come away transformed for the future. As one who served two tours in that conflict, I highly recommend this work to the American people.

Al Maxey, Petty Officer 3rd Class
Vietnam, 1969-1971

Life on a Short Fuse

AN AMERICAN FIGHTER PILOT REVEALS
A MILITARY COVER-UP RESPONSIBLE FOR MORE THAN
20 DEATHS
AND UNSPEAKABLE TORTURE

Lt. Col. Jack L. Drain
USAF Retired

Foreword by
Col. Thomas N. Moe

**My Life
on
Loan**

BEDFORD, TEXAS

Published by My Life on Loan, Inc., 733 Hunters Glen Court, Bedford, TX 76021. www.MyLifeOnLoan.com.

My Life on Loan is a 501 (c)(3) nonprofit organization. Profits from the publication of its books and products will primarily be donated to charitable groups as the board may approve.

Published with the assistance of Creative Enterprises Ltd., 1507 Shirley Way, Bedford, TX 76022. www.CreativeEnterprisesLtd.com

Unless otherwise noted, Scripture quotations are from the Holy Bible, New International Version (NIV). Copyright © 1973, 1978, 1984, International Bible Society. Used by permission of Zondervan Bible Publishers.

Quotations designated NCV are from the New Century Version®. Copyright © 1987, 1988, 1991 by Thomas Nelson, Inc. All rights reserved.

Interior design: Inside Out Design & Typesetting, Hurst, TX.

Cover design: www.thedugandesigngroup.com

Printed in the United States of America.

ISBN 978-0-9819683-0-8

09 10 11 12 13 14 15 16   MP   8 7 6 5 4 3 2 1

The Series

Welcome to a new series of books and media presentations, each conveying the eternal premise that we have nothing we can truly call our own. Instead the earth and all its inhabitants were created by God and belong to Him. Our lives are "but a vapor" in the grand scheme of things, but oh! what a whisk it is for us and those around us as we vaporize together. Someday we will all be asked for an accounting of what was given to us and what we did with it. We believe we need to prepare to give that accounting before the final curtain call when the trumpets, harps, and angelic choirs silence our audience before the Great I AM.

We are the clients, not the Judge. We are the specimens under the microscope, not the Scientist. We are the sheep, not the Shepherd. We are the servants, not the Master. Yet we are so valuable to God that His only Son died so we can have eternal life.

Do we preach any sermons while we live? Yes, we do! Every day of our lives someone is learning something because of *who we are* more than because of *what we do*. No one dies who has not influenced another . . . either for good or evil.

That being the foundation of this effort, we seek to prepare for the coming accounting and lay out our stories for those who will follow us in their own God-given plans. "Why do this?" you ask. Read this book carefully, and we believe the answer will become clear to you just as it has for us. Look not for a single answer but for the golden threads woven into life's tapestry by the Master while we were not looking.

THE PUBLISHER

In Germany they came first for the communists; I did not speak out because I was not a communist. Then they came for the Jews; I did not speak because I was not a Jew. Then they came to fetch the workers, members of the trade unions; I did not speak because I was not a trade unionist. Afterward they came for the Catholics; I did not say anything because I was a Protestant. Eventually they came for me, and there was no one left to speak.

Martin Niemoller
"First They Came"
They Thought They Were Free

Contents

Foreword

War is a horrible undertaking, no matter what the cause for which it is fought. But of all the ills that accompany war—suffering, death, and destruction—among the vilest is betrayal. Betrayal cuts so deeply because victory, nay survival itself, rests on trust. A citizenry trusts its warriors; the warrior in turn trusts completely his comrades and the means given him to destroy the threat—his equipment. The insult of betrayal is doubled when the defects of equipment are known and/or perpetuated by politics or profit—the two usually go hand in hand.

This is the true story of such a betrayal and how it destroyed so many valiant men and their families. Their sacrifice, in the face of this betrayal, is made even more poignant given the disregard shown by those in authority who had the knowledge and means to rectify the situation . . . but did nothing.

The events in this story took place long ago. The telling of the story honors, at long last, those who lost their lives because of defective bomb fuses. We knew that many planes and their pilots had been lost because of the fuse defect, but we could not prove it. A hiatus on carrying the fuses was ordered by our deputy of operations, apparently without the approval of his doubting superiors, and an attempt was made during that time to determine whether there was a fuse problem or not.

None found, we resumed carrying the fuses, and I was scheduled to fly on the ill-fated mission. But I survived the explosion that occurred during bomb release, and I was able to contact another flight with my eyewitness account as I descended in my parachute into enemy territory. It was the first time we had irrefutable evidence of the fuse problem. The pilot I contacted immediately radioed headquarters, which ordered that the fuse be quarantined, and other flights that were already on their way to certain destruction be recalled.

Now turn the pages as my friend Jack Drain recounts for you the sad story in detail, including my own story of capture and incarceration as a POW for more than five horrifying years. I am forever grateful for his dogged determination to put the pieces of this tragic puzzle together, even though we still don't have the final piece of the puzzle—the fundamental defect in the fuse that shattered so many lives.

Thomas N. Moe, Colonel USAF (retired)
Lancaster, Ohio

Acknowledgments

This book would not be possible without recognizing the loving protection of God and His guardian angels. Nor would it have been achieved without the comments of Jerry Stephens, Michael Brinkley, my wife, Carolyn, and many others. They saw it in the unedited form and believed in it.

Next would be Pat Nimmo Riddle, longtime respected feature writer for the *Fort Worth Star-Telegram*, who painstakingly did the first edit of this manuscript. Thanks for everything, Pat!

A special thanks to Tom Moe for sharing his story and providing essential details.

Finally Mary Hollingsworth, who was willing to take it on and do the professional editing, project management, and obtain the services of the following talented people: Rhonda Hogan for the legalities, Kathryn Murray for interior design and typesetting, Patty Crowley and Stephanie Terry for proofreading, Tom Williams and Dugan Design Group for cover design, and Roger Demaree for production and printing.

Thank you all!

To God be the glory.

Introduction: The Dead Cry Out!

The first draft for this book was created under the title *Friendly Fire* in 2002, and a copy was filed with the National Archives for the Vietnam War at Texas Tech University in Lubbock, Texas. It was never published beyond my family and a few close friends.

At that time Col. Thomas N. Moe, who was in my squadron from 1967–1968 in Danang, Vietnam, intended to coauthor the book. At the end of my tour, I was fortunate to come home to my wife, Carolyn, and children. Unfortunately, then "Lieutenant" Moe stayed in Vietnam as a prisoner of war (POW). I have not seen Moe since 1968, and truthfully we were not really close friends then. I wrote my half of the book, but for many reasons, including the demands of life, Moe was not able to write his half. I do have his powerful POW account, however, and it is included here with his permission.

We set out determined to combine our efforts in a book about personal experiences before, during, and after Vietnam. Our hope was that writing it would help us find peace on behalf of our fallen comrades, encourage Vietnam veterans still living, and help explain why tragedy has befallen tens of thousands of other Vietnam veterans.

Even though the Vietnam War Memorial in Washington, DC, has 58,191 names engraved on it, alarming statistics show that many more have committed suicide, and from 100,000 to 200,000 have been incarcerated in America's prisons with even more likely on parole. One study showed that one in four Vietnam vets had been arrested for a criminal offense. From a known number of 147 Vietnam vets on Death Row, the number might actually be more than 200. About 14 percent of those who served in Vietnam (one in seven) still have serious psychological problems, and of this group 70 percent have been divorced at least once, including Senator John McCain, who was unable to sustain his marriage after his long incarceration. Other statistics are shocking and sobering as shown in the following chart.

Statistics about the Vietnam War

From Mary Kinsey, JMU Department of Integrated Science and Technology, and Vietnam Veterans of America, Speakers Bureau Handbook *provided by the Public Affairs Committee.*

- 61 percent of the men who were killed in the Vietnam War were twenty-one years of age or younger.
- The Vietnam War lasted sixteen years (1959 to 1975).
- The state of West Virginia had the highest death rate, based on a per capita population, with 81 percent. The national average was 58.9 percent for every 100,000 males.
- Only 25 percent of the total United States forces serving in Vietnam were draftees as compared to 66 percent during World War II.
- Approximately 2,031 people were missing in action during the Vietnam War—766 were POWs and 114 died in captivity.
- The educational level of the draftees during the Vietnam War breaks down as 79 percent had high school or higher educations; 76 percent of these were from lower middle/working-class families.
- The average age of the soldiers serving during the Vietnam War was nineteen. The average age of the soldiers serving during World War II was twenty-six.
- Approximately 97 percent of Vietnam Veterans were honorably discharged.
- Approximately 66 percent of Vietnam Veterans have said that they were proud of the time in service and what they did during the Vietnam War.
- Approximately 87 percent of the general public now hold Vietnam Veterans in high esteem.

- Vietnam Veterans make up 9.7 percent of their generation.
- 9,087,000 military personnel served on active duty during the Vietnam Era (5 August 1964 through 7 May 1975).
- 8,744,000 personnel were on active duty during the war (5 August 1964 through 28 March 1973).
- 3,403,100 (including an additional 514,000 offshore) served in the Southeast Asia Theater, which included Vietnam, Laos, Cambodia, flight crews based in Thailand, and sailors in adjacent South China Sea waters.
- 2,594,000 personnel served within the borders of South Vietnam (1 January 1965 to 28 March 1973).
- Another 50,000 men served in Vietnam between 1960 and 1964.
- Of the 2.6 million personnel who served within the borders of South Vietnam, 40 percent to 60 percent either fought in combat, provided close combat support, or were at least fairly regularly exposed to enemy attack.
- 7,484 women served in Vietnam; 6,250 (approximately 83.5 percent) were nurses.
- Peak troop strength in Vietnam was 543,482 (30 April 1969).
- There were 47,359 hostile deaths.
- There were 10,797 non-hostile deaths.
- Total of 58,156 (which includes men formerly classified as MIA and Mayaguez casualties). Twenty-seven additional men have died of wounds sustained in the Vietnam War, which brings the death total to 58,183.
- 8 nurses died in Vietnam—one was Killed In Action.
- 17,539 of the men killed in Vietnam were married.
- 303,704 personnel were wounded—153,329 were hospitalized and 150,375 required no hospital care.
- 88.4 percent of the men who actually served in Vietnam were Caucasian.
- 10.6 percent of the men who actually served in Vietnam were Black.
- 1 percent of the men who actually served in Vietnam were of other races.
- 86.3 percent of the men who died in Vietnam were Caucasian (includes Hispanics).
- 12.5 percent of the men who died in Vietnam were Black.
- 1.2 percent of the men who died in Vietnam were of other races.
- 170,000 Hispanics served in Vietnam. Of that total, 3,070 (5.2 percent of the total) died there.
- 34 percent of the Blacks who enlisted, volunteered for combat duty.

> **The Vietnamese people also suffered severe losses:**
> - More than 200,000 South Vietnamese troops died.
> - More than a million Vietnamese civilians died.
> - There were more than 6.5 million displaced war refugees.
>
> *World Almanac and Book of Facts, 1998 (World Almanac Books: 1997)*

People need so badly to understand that the dead cry out to us. I am also a veteran of the Korean conflict of the 1950s. Moe was taken prisoner in 1968 and spent the next five years in a North Vietnamese prison camp. Some experiences included in this story have waited more than forty years to be revealed in print. By doing this now, I hope to encourage others to come forth with their own personal stories. Time is running out for all of us. Memories are fading, and the clarity of our minds might soon be tested.

Some of the story I will be adding to was covered very well in Lynda Twyman Paffrath's book *Angels Unknown*,[1] available from Amazon.com. I plan to raise the bar on questions without answers.

A quick check of this book's original title, *Friendly Fire,* on the Internet pulls up hundreds of materials that have absolutely nothing to do with what will be discussed here. Tom Moe and I had a cause we hoped to share with a nation of people who care about the past, present, and future. The subject reaches the most sensitive cores of our very beings. You can call it "friendly fire" or a "cover-up," but it has to do with the self-destruction of our internal processes, whether physical or mental. This is not just a military problem; it is a disease of our world, our nation, and our homes, with the seeds planted deep in all of us. It's called "hiding the truth." We had it in Watergate, Monicagate, Infidelitygate, and in Traitorgate—the story of John Walker. Whether we recognize it or not, we live with it, some of us better than others. For me, it has been longer than most. We have, at one time or another, failed each other, and even worse we've failed ourselves.

Vietnam was a place where America found many hidden weaknesses and chinks in her armor. Not every citizen is a patriot. Not every citizen is honorable. Not every citizen is dependable or reliable in a time of crisis. We do not want the history books to remember the Vietnam *protesters* without the American *protectors*—those valiant people who believed and died doing what was asked of them by our country. The success of the movie *We Were Soldiers* indicates that Americans are now ready to deal with the events and details of that horrible conflict. Perhaps, finally, we can recognize that good can arise like the phoenix from the ashes of greed, arrogance, and ignorance. We all received a lesson in humility.

Marine Lt. Col. Oliver North in his book *One More Mission* offers five possibilities to explain why there is such a disturbing record for the Vietnam vets known as the "walking wasted":

1. Vietnam was the first war we had ever lost.

2. The only ones "welcomed home" were the prisoners of war.

3. More of the severely wounded survived due to the excellent medical care they received.

4. They spent more days in the direct line of fire than soldiers in other wars.

5. It was a different mix of American men: younger, poorer, and in some cases less competent than those in previous wars.[2]

McNamara's Project 100,000

In 1966 Secretary of Defense Robert S. McNamara initiated what came to be called by other military personnel the "Moron Corps." Called a "great society program," McNamara's Project 100,000 lowered the military enlistment requirements to recruit 100,000 men per year—men who sadly had marginal minds and bodies. Recruiters swept through urban ghettos and the southern hill country, taking some young men with IQs below what is considered legally retarded.

In all some 354,000 men volunteered for Project 100,000. Until that time, the minimum passing score on the armed forces qualification test had been 31 out of 100. Under McNamara's Project 100,000, those who scored as low as 10 were taken, if they lived in a specified poverty area. In 1969 out of 120 U. S. Marine Corps volunteers from Oakland, California, nearly 90 percent scored under 31; more than 70 percent were African American or Hispanic. Overall 41 percent of Project 100,000 volunteers were African American, compared to 12 percent of the rest of the armed forces. Claiming to provide rehabilitation, remedial education, and an escape from poverty, the program actually provided a front seat on the bus to Vietnam, where they fought and died in disproportionate numbers. The advertised skills and training were seldom really taught.

McNamara called these men the "subterranean poor," as if they lived in caves. In a way they did, because their pathetic ghettos and pitiful hill towns were never seen by America's wealthy. But that was good for McNamara and his president, Lyndon Johnson. Project 100,000 never mentioned that the Moron Corps provided the needed military personnel to help evade the politically dangerous necessity of dropping student deferments or calling up the reserves, which were hideouts for the wealthy.

While government officials denied that the Moron Corps were dying in higher numbers than other military, the undeniable statistics say something entirely different. In fact, 40 percent of Project 100,000 men were trained for combat, compared with 25 percent of general service personnel. In one 1969 evaluation of Project 100,000, the Department of Defense put the attrition-by-death rate at 1.1 percent. By contrast, the overall death rate for Vietnam-era veterans was only 0.6 percent.

Taken from public facts on file.

Introduction

According to historian Victor Davis Hanson:

The vast majority of those who fought in Vietnam as front-line combat troops—two thirds of whom were not drafted but volunteered—were disproportionately lower-income whites from southern and rural states. These were young men of a vastly different socioeconomic cosmos from the largely middle- and upper-class journalists, who misrepresented them, the antiwar activists and academics who castigated them, and the generals of the military high command who led them so poorly.[3]

There is much of this war that begs to be silenced, because it was a disaster in so many ways. We were caught up in World War II, the Soviet threat, and Korean-styled diplomacy. It was disastrously unique. Here's a good analogy of Vietnam: Suppose the Democrats and the Republicans declare war on each other in America. The Canadians support the Democrats, and the Vietnamese support the Republicans. There are no battle lines, as the combatants are intermingled. To the Vietnamese all Americans look alike, speak the same language, and have the same heritage. To add to the confusion, many years ago a corrupt British government pulled out, leaving behind a flimsy civil servant cadre of rulers who had learned the ways of bribery and pay-offs. The majority of the population had never voted for a political figure and unquestioningly accepted whatever came their way with greed and apathy. They fought the war with the same attitude. How would you (the Vietnamese) win?

One way we tried to win was by using the World War II tactic of overwhelming material support. In the harbor at Danang, forty to seventy ships were always anchored, waiting their turns at the docks to unload and return to the United States. This continued for more than ten years.

The ships unloaded twenty-four hours a day, seven days a week. The bomb and flare dumps were stretched to capacity. Missions were flown around the clock to use up the supplies so that more fuel, more bombs, more rockets, napalm, weapons, Jeeps, trucks, artillery, and fuses could be unloaded. To compound the issue, Danang was not the only seaport, and the same tactics were used everywhere. An in-depth study of this ridiculous scenario can be found in *A Decent Interval*,[4] written by Central Intelligence Agency (CIA) agent Frank Snepp, who was in Vietnam through the entire conflict until its horrible end. These are incredible stories! Even though it is now out of print, copies can still be found.

Another way we tried to win was the Air Superiority theory of WWII. The theory was that, if we controlled the skies, we could control the ground. We did that! We had absolute domination of the skies over South Vietnam, and enemy aircraft did not prevent us from having access to any area of the North. Political decisions, not military ones, controlled the skies of North Vietnam. The introduction of surface-to-air missiles (SAMs)—antiaircraft weapons on the ground—played havoc with our air superiority, increasing the price paid, but it did not curtail our capabilities.

Tom Moe and I had unique stories to relate from this ill-conceived war. Our lives were different then, and they still are. Neither of us fit the picture of a Vietnam veteran as described by Oliver North. We have not seen each other since January 1968. I am older than Tom. I completed a one-hundred-mission tour flying F-84s in the Korean War while Tom was still in grade school. I was a major and Tom a lieutenant when we were flying F-4s in Vietnam. Tom trained for Vietnam at Davis-Monthan Air Force Base near Tucson, Arizona. I went through George AFB near Victorville and Apple Valley, California. It has been a long time since our paths first crossed. I did not know if we ever flew together until I asked Tom, but he does not think so.

Introduction

I sent the above information to Tom for a draft reading, and his response was, "Great work, Jack, only 500 pages to go. I don't think we ever flew together, but I'd fly your wing anytime." What a great compliment from a furnace-tested veteran. I wrote him back and advised him, "No, I only have 247.5 pages to go, and you have 250." The conversation quickly turned into a discussion of filling up the 500 pages. Jokingly, we agreed that we would use "lots of quotations, pictures, and statistics which we would make up on the spot."

I still believe we shared a cause. We also had a purpose. I want to reach all individuals who harbor tragic secrets and wonder if they are alone. I hope that by sharing stories (and those of the people we have contacted) we can better understand the built-in human condition best described as *survival*. And you, dear reader, should know that I am also telling your story, as you vicariously experience what we did. At the end of each segment of the book, ask yourself, How would I have responded in that situation? Perhaps then you will come closer to feeling and experiencing what we did.

I challenged myself to find out why most of my friends in the war turned out differently from the veterans' statistics in the Oliver North report. Most did not commit suicide, have not been in prison or on parole, did not divorce their wives, and while they may have needed mental counseling, they did not seek it. They are not in the "walking wasted" category. I invite you to join me on this life journey as we attempt to answer the question, Why not?

JACK DRAIN

Prologue:
On a Wing and a Prayer

In Vietnam Capt. Richard "Red" Whitteker and I flew most of our missions together, but it wasn't unusual to mix crews. My fiftieth mission was flown with Lt. Joe Koziusko, now just called Joe Koz. We were diverted from our original target by bad weather and were released to find a target of our own. I don't remember the call sign for the flight, but we were No. 1, and the other plane was No. 2. I decided to work over a group of buildings along a bend on a riverbank that might be used for storage of supplies during the day. We each had Gatling guns and 250-pound bombs. We released the bombs on the first pass and then made several passes with the guns. Several buildings were burning, and we saw a few secondary explosions. I had not been aware of any significant ground fire in our direction.

When I pulled off from the last pass, I headed toward the sea, as a line of shells popped up right in front of the aircraft. We took one in the right wing. I knew it was bad when lights began flashing amber and red in the cockpit. I fire-walled the throttles in afterburner and climbed out toward the sea to eject, as I was pretty sure we were not going to be able to stay in the air. I called the No. 2 plane to come with us to see if they could see the damage. We still had controls, and both engines were running, so I headed south toward Danang.

No. 2 pulled up under us and I asked, "How bad is it?" We could not see anything from the cockpit.

The pilot said, "You've got a large hole just behind the leading edge of the wing, and fuel is streaming out. It looks like there are lots of smaller holes in the fuselage as well. The main hole is about three feet from the fuselage. We'll stay with you."

Joe advised me he was okay and gave me a heading for home. I had already issued a Mayday call, and as long as we were in control, I was determined to get the plane back. The choppers were already airborne toward our route of flight. We streamed fuel all the way back to the base, and I made a flaps-up, straight-in landing approach. I put the tail hook down and took the center cable to stop the airplane.

The fire trucks were on the edge of the runway where we stopped, but they were not needed. When we got out, we saw a hole thirty-six inches long and twenty-nine inches wide just in front of the main wing spar. Fuel and hydraulic fluid dripped from a dozen holes and lines. The plane was towed to the line for a few days and then to a hangar where it stayed for three months. A team of people came from the factory and repaired it enough for a flight back to the States and a wing change. I have a photo of the damaged plane.

I was already scheduled for an R & R trip to Hong Kong after that flight, and I took it! On the ride to Hong Kong, how close I came to dying finally hit me. I was a basket case for about an hour. Joe kept on flying missions as if nothing had happened. And me? I added another cluster to God's Distinguished Flying Cross, because it belonged to Him. I just considered it on loan to me.

During the rest of that flight, I reflected on my life and what unusual events and adventures had brought me to that terrifying day.

PART 1

Flying with Angels

For [God] will command his angels

concerning you to guard you in all your ways;

they will lift you up in their hands,

so that you will not strike your foot

against a stone.

PSALM 91:11–12

1 From Room 2 to F-4s

Florence Nightingale Hospital
Dallas, Texas
28 April 1929

I've always told my children I was born in room 2 of the Florence Nightingale Hospital. I think that was the earlier name in 1929 for Baylor Hospital in Dallas, Texas. The Great Depression was in full swing, and my dad was not able to find work. We moved in with my grandparents on their farm outside of Edgewood, which is about forty-five miles east of Dallas.

It is hard for me to know the difference between what I *remember* and what I was *told* about those years. I do recall the embarrassing Saturday evening baths in a No. 2 washtub on the back porch of the "big house." All the workers from the fields came by laughing and shouting some kind of greeting as my mother bent over me with a soapy rag. Two "colored" families lived in private homes on the farmland. I had much fun playing with their children in the cotton fields or breaking open a watermelon out in the hot sun. We had fields full of melons that sold for almost nothing at the market.

Just before I turned school age, we moved back to a small rent house in Dallas. I fell in love in the first or second grade with a Shirley Temple look-alike. Several years later my family moved in with my aunt and uncle to care for them after they had a serious automobile accident, causing broken bones and other slow-recovery injuries. Early one Christmas morning near the end of that nursing assignment, we received a call that Grandfather Livingston had died. We had not opened our presents, and we packed quickly for the trip back to Edgewood, leaving all our presents behind unopened. We stayed a week, and I was doubly grieved, both for my grandfather and my presents. Grandfather had a gift for me—a pocket knife. I was very proud of it.

On to Vickery

After Aunt Zelma Wilson and Uncle Norman recovered, we moved to a small but clean rental house in Vickery, Texas, then a suburb but now a part of Dallas. It was an idyllic place in my mind, as there were open fields, deep woods, and a swimming hole in White Rock Creek. I spent many blissful hours playing "scrub" baseball, bike riding, having mud-ball fights, participating in Cub and Boy Scouts, digging a hole to China, and riding the interurban to downtown Dallas for double-feature movies.

I finished grade school and most of high school in Vickery before moving back into Dallas, where I rode to and from school with one of our teachers. I spent my freshman and sophomore years at Vickery-Hillcrest, which is now a very large school called Hillcrest High School. I had a crush on Ganelle in grade school and Miriam in high school.

One afternoon in high school, playing baseball, I broke my right wrist. One of the teachers took me to downtown Dallas, had my arm x-rayed and set in a cast that went from my hand to halfway between my elbow and shoulder, and brought me back to school. I rode the bus home and walked into the kitchen where my mother nearly fainted when she saw me. I just can't imagine that happening today.

4

My dad had a Model A Ford that I used for dating. We had thirty-six students in our senior class and one hundred forty-four in the total high school. I took part in many activities to cover all the bases. I played football, joined the band, worked on the yearbooks, acted in or supported all the drama plays, and was a trainer for the basketball team, since all my friends were more than six-feet tall. Some nights I worked at the A & P grocery store. In addition, I threw a morning paper route on my bicycle, worked one summer for a fruit and vegetable stand, and spent another summer as a "drag-off" boy behind a hay bailing crew. While all bailed, I stacked four hundred bales a day, six days a week. Each bale weighed from seventy to ninety pounds, so I was ready for some easy times when football season came the fall of my junior year; I played right guard. In the band I played the French horn.

We had some of the finest teachers in the world. Coach Killough was a great man and a good friend to all of us.

I had a problem keeping my mouth shut during class lectures. My outbursts eventually exasperated my teacher, Mrs. Graham. After one of my frivolous comments brought a laughing response from the class, she slowly and silently walked over in front of my desk, waited until the silence was deafening, then said, "I wish I could buy you for what you are worth and sell you for what you *think* you are worth. I would be a very rich woman." Obviously I have never forgotten that moment of truth.

Texas Tech

We were the last of a group that attended eleven years of school. I graduated one month after my seventeenth birthday and went to Texas Tech University the following fall. To get to Lubbock from Dallas you have to drive through Fort Worth. When I went to college, I recall entering Fort Worth for the first time even though it is only thirty-two miles from

Dallas. At that point I had been to Galveston and Chicago but never to Fort Worth.

With a room off campus in Lubbock, I worked at odd jobs more than I attended classes in order to pay my expenses and eat regularly. Tuition at the state school was twenty-five dollars a semester for all the hours you could carry. I started college with three hundred fifty dollars and stretched it as far as it would go. One summer and fall I worked in a labor gang for Illinois Natural Gas at a high-pressure pipeline pumping station in the Texas Panhandle. From the other laborers I learned how to pace my work to last all day at our grueling tasks. I lived in Borger, Texas, met Miss Borger, and was "pinned" to her by the time I returned to school. She soon lost out, though, to a girl named Carolyn.

Lackland Air Force Base
San Antonio, Texas
28 December 1950

By the fall of 1950 I had missed two semesters, and the draft was breathing down my neck, so I applied for aviation cadet training in the summer and had a four-month deferment waiting for a class assignment. On December 28, 1950, I went to the U. S. Air Force recruiting office in downtown Dallas and started the enlistment process to keep my cadet application intact while I waited for a class. We took tests and filled out forms for several hours. They had a bus take us to Love Field for the physicals. I had the Model-A, so I drove there behind the bus. About eight o'clock that evening we were sworn in, and they said a bus would be there shortly to take us to Lackland Air Force Base near San Antonio, Texas. I just had time to call Dad and tell him that I would leave the keys on the floor of the car, and he would have to come and get it.

I was now worth ten thousand dollars . . . if I died.

Lackland was a nightmare in early 1951. Buses arrived, steadily bringing recruits from all over the country. (I heard figures of 85,000 to 100,000). Our flight was housed in a classroom with no toilet facilities. Thousands of others

I was now worth ten thousand dollars . . . if I died.

were camped out on the fields in tents, and the last ones to arrive were sent to the baseball field to sleep on the ground (uncovered). They were able to feed everyone, but most did not have uniforms or were missing many articles of clothing. Some of our guys marched in their civilian cowboy boots for weeks.

After two weeks I was helping pitch tents when someone came from the squadron office for me. They confirmed that I was a cadet applicant and reassigned me to one of the training squadrons. I was issued a complete uniform, housed in a barracks, and given a three-day weekend pass. When I returned from visiting my girlfriend, Carolyn Burgess, in Lubbock, they sent me to school for two weeks on base to become a "career guidance counselor."

I spent the next five months sending recruits to their assignments all over America. Women were just beginning to enter the armed forces in large numbers about that time. When I had to tell each one that she could not be a "flight attendant," she usually cried, and the lieutenant in charge came over to help me explain the facts of military life. It was a tough job, but someone had to do it! I was making ninety-four dollars a month and able to save some of it.

TERRIFIED BY A T-6

Orders for Class 52-D came, and I went to Bartow, Florida, in June 1951. It was a start-up pilot training base, and we were the first class. The

7

officers acted as upperclassmen and set the rituals for us to follow, as we trained those behind us. It was very much like West Point.

We had civilian flight instructors, and I was assigned to Bo Shuford. On the first flight he set out to demonstrate what a good pilot he was, as well as the maneuverability of a great aircraft like the T-6. He nearly scared me to death! A T-6 is a single-engine propeller aircraft with tandem seating. Many of the Japanese Zeros in the movies are really T-6s.

> **My fear of flying was to last for twenty-one more years.**

My fear of flying was to last for twenty-one more years. After living through that ride, I made up my mind that they could not make it too rough for me and that I could take everything they dished out. It was an attitude that helped me endure many rugged times when I really wanted to cut and run. Most of us felt that way.

After six months of primary training, we moved on to Perrin AFB, Texas (near Sherman), for training in the new T-28, a propeller aircraft of amazing speed, power, and agility after flying the T-6. I scared the fool out of myself again doing night acrobatics . . . solo! Lights on the ground can look a lot like stars when you are twirling around in the dark skies. This time we had military instructors. They were younger and less experienced than our civilian teachers, and we were the first class at Perrin. Incidentally, during World War II my father had worked as a carpenter, building the barracks where we stayed at Perrin.

WINGS, BARS, AND NARROW ESCAPES

Three months whizzed by, then we progressed as the first class at Webb AFB in Big Spring, Texas, flying T-33 jets. I was also closer to my sweetheart, Carolyn. My Uncle Lonnie loaned me a Dodge coupe, and I kept the tires spinning between Big Spring and Lubbock. We graduated on June 25, 1952, receiving our silver pilots' wings and gold second-lieu-tenant bars. When Carolyn pinned the wings and bars on me, I was one proud cookie. We had been told for a solid year that we were the cream of the crop of American young men, and finally I think we believed it.

Carolyn and I became engaged the summer before I left for gunnery school at Luke AFB near Phoenix, Arizona. Roughly half of the class went to F-84 training at Luke, while the others went to F-86 training at Nellis AFB near Las Vegas, Nevada. Almost all of the class had orders to go to Korea after temporary duty at the two schools.

We were by no means the first class at Luke. We were training in worn-out F-84 B and C models, which had seen too many flights and were miss-ing too many parts. During the ninety-day training, I had three incidents or accidents that had life-endangering potential. On one gunnery mission a hydraulic line rupture in my cockpit right after I pulled off and up from a strafing run at the Gila Bend Range, southwest of Luke. I was covered by a fine mist of hot, slick hydraulic fluid, as were the cockpit instruments, controls, and switches. The canopy filled with mist like smoke and glazed the plastic windshield and visor, seriously blurring my vision.

Gila Bend had a short airstrip, and I elected to put the aircraft down there rather than try to reach the home field some forty-five miles away. Everything went well until I attempted to land. In that airplane the loss of hydraulic power meant a loss of hydraulic struts on the wheels. When they bottomed out after touchdown the aircraft bounced back up in the air about fifteen feet. Since the airspeed was now so low that it was no longer able to fly, it dropped like a rock, driving the struts up into the wings and giving me one whale of a jolt. Standing on the brakes I was able to get the aircraft stopped some ten feet from the end of the runway. I opened the canopy, and the fireman from the range helped me out, so we could leave the plane as soon as possible in case of fire. Because it was an early summer afternoon in the desert, I soon was in misery from the sun boiling down on my oil-soaked flight suit. They took me to their station, and I got in the shower to undress and get the oil off my body. They loaned me some clothes, and a helicopter from Luke came to take me home.

Another day we had finished our training flight and were taxiing in from the runway on the perimeter of the field. As I applied the brakes to slow down to make a turn, the left brake worked, but the right one did not, and the aircraft turned back toward the active runway. In order to keep the aircraft from going onto a runway in front of other aircraft on takeoff roll, I ground-looped the plane with the left brake. Meanwhile the ruptured hydraulic line on the right wheel was squirting oil on the hot brake, and it caught on fire. One of the pilots on the takeoff roll advised me of the fire and said to stop and get out immediately. I did, and the plane was engulfed by fire by the time the base firefighters arrived.

Shortly before we finished our training, the base received the first F-84 G model planes. To celebrate the end of training, they let six of us take the aircraft on a weekend trip around the United States. About dark we took off, circled Las Vegas, flew over San Francisco, and headed toward Norton AFB near San Bernardino, California. The smog was so bad we could only see the field when directly over it. We came down in two formations, peeled off over the end of the runway and began landing one right after the other. I was the last to land.

As I touched down I heard the tower giving taxi instructions to the planes in front of me. Two of them had missed a turn-off point and had turned around on the active runway, *headed toward me*. I didn't have enough room to take off again, so to avoid a head-on collision, I tried to turn off on a crossing runway to the left. I misjudged my speed and location and turned too soon, shearing off the left wheel and hitting their high-intensity runway lights. I slid down the cross runway about a thousand feet as the field went completely dark. Surprisingly uninjured, I opened the canopy, stepped out on the ground, and walked away.

Surprisingly uninjured, I opened the canopy, stepped out on the ground, and walked away.

I had not gone very far when vehicles started coming onto the runways from all directions. Some guy ran past me and muttered, "We can't find the pilot." I called out to him that I was the pilot, and he came back and looked at me with his flashlight.

I said, "See? I have a parachute on my back; I'm the pilot."

He took me by the arm and rushed me to an old WWII ambulance. I told him I was not hurt, but he insisted that I had to get checked out at the base hospital. I crawled in the passenger side of the ambulance, and we drove off. There was another vehicle behind us, honking constantly.

We finally pulled over, and a brand new ambulance pulled alongside the driver and asked, "Do you have the pilot?"

The driver informed them he did, and they began to argue about who was going to take me to the hospital. I thought the whole situation was hilarious! When my driver realized I was laughing so hard at them, he stiffened and furiously drove on to the hospital.

The rest of the group left the following morning to complete the trip, but I was required to stay for the next ten days while the accident was investigated. This time the base sent a B-25 after me, and I rode back to Luke in the nose of the plane, which a bombardier would have formerly occupied. I even got to log some flying time in that plane.

By the time I returned to base, my class was already gone, except for one member, Johnny Evans, whom I visited in the base hospital. He had been forced to land a flamed-out F-84 in the desert, badly injuring his back. I visited with him several years ago, and he is still not certain whether he was hurt in the rough landing or in the exertion it took to get the canopy open when the plane caught fire. At the end of his ride, he said he met "a boulder that refused to get out of the way."

I packed my bags and went home on leave before heading to Korea.

2 The First Hundred Missions

K-2 Airfield
Taegu, Korea
November 1952

On my way to Korea, I had to make one more stop, this time in San Francisco. If there is one thing I know about the military, there is nothing subtle about their motives. I spent twelve days learning how to be a prisoner of war. Talk about a morale booster! I would have to kill you if I told you about the school, but it was a doozie. I did get to log some flying time in a Catalina Flying Boat, and I found out what it was like to land on water.

We flew from San Francisco to Alaska and then on to Japan, a long flight in a propeller aircraft. I spent a few days in Japan, and then a C-47 took me to Taegu, Korea. K-2 was the military airfield designation.

Except for a few ferry trips to Japan and a week's stay on the front lines, I spent most of the next nine months getting in my one hundred missions in the F-84.

We lived in a barracks across the "Green Nile" from the Officer's Club. The Green Nile was a stagnate twelve-foot-wide body of water where our houseboy, Kim, washed our clothes. There was a bridge crossing, and it was clearly understood by all that should anyone fall in, someone was to take out his forty-five and shoot him. Well, not really, but the odor was horrible, and we jokingly agreed we would rather die than fall into it.

A Traditional War

Korea was a traditional war. We knew where the enemy was, and there were clear lines of "real estate" belonging to each side. It had been in a more fluid state earlier on, but by the time I arrived, no one was eager to capture more land. The cost was simply too high.

We flew mostly in the daytime in good weather. Strategic bombing by mass gaggles of aircraft was common. Sometimes as many as ninety-six aircraft would rise from several airfields, and we would reach far north of the thirty-eighth parallel to strike bridges, dams, and industrial centers. A full load of bombs and fuel in the F-84 meant adding a Jet-Assisted Take Off (JATO) bottle to the bottom of the plane to get airborne. About a mile off the end of the runway was a JATO drop area for the expended bottle. The area was usually occupied by many Korean nationals who wanted the metal casings to make things they could sell to the troops. It has always been a mystery to me how they managed to dodge the falling three-foot-long, eighty-five-pound bottles.

These mass aircraft flights had some serious drawbacks. It took hours to get all of them on the bomb run in single file. Some were targeting the antiaircraft guns, and some were bombing the bridges or dams. To get in and get out without running into each other or flying through another plane's bombs, we set up a pattern. It didn't take the enemy long to know exactly what we were doing, and they set up their flak patterns to respond accordingly. We could see the pattern for fifty miles before reaching the area. It was outlined by the flak for us to fly through. We hoped they would run out of ammo by the time we arrived, but no such luck. We would lose several aircraft and pilots before we finished each trip.

At this stage, I added the fear of flak to my fear of flying.

We would change altitudes and the flak would follow us, so we knew they had some radar tracking sites and guns. After returning from one of those missions and parking on the designated painted square for the nose wheel, I saw my crew chief dart under the airplane after placing the chocks. He came back out shaking his head and holding his arms out, palms up in disbelief. I dismounted and took a look for myself. In the very center of my extended speed brake was a four-inch hole where a shell had gone through and not exploded. I must have been on the dive bomb run when a gunner in line with my flight fired directly at me. Why it didn't explode, I'll never know. I know that my bombs went off on top of him or mighty close to his site. I could see them as I pulled away from the target. Once the bombs left the aircraft, we jinked like crazy to get away from the flak area.

For my nonmilitary readers, *jinked* means to fly the aircraft erratically, changing course and altitude rapidly. The purpose is to prevent an enemy gunner from being able to project a flight path and then aim at a spot where the plane *will be* when the bullets or shells arrive there.

The air force picked that mission to give me a Distinguished Flying Cross. I'll pass the honor on to God, who obviously protected me.

NIGHT INTRUDER MISSIONS

As scary as the day missions were, the night solo missions struck a new high in terror. These were called "night intruder" missions. The purpose was to keep enemy trucks from using their headlights while bringing supplies to the front and to disrupt their sleeping.

Weather was a powerful factor in our conduct of this mission. We flew hundreds of miles north of the parallel, let down through the clouds, and broke out into a totally black night. There were no lights on the ground and none in the sky. We dimmed our cockpit lights to the point where we could barely see our instruments and started searching for a glimmer or string of lights from hooded headlamps on the enemies' trucks below. Finding them, we would throttle back and try to glide in close enough to drop bombs along their route. Much of North Korea is very hilly, and when they knew we were there, they would turn off their lights. We hoped the sudden darkness would cause them not to be able to see the road, drive off the edge, and roll down the side of a hill. Frankly, this "war tactic" still sounds as unbelievably corny to me now as it did then.

That was the plan, but what actually happened was a little different. The strings of dim lights were hard to find, and we usually searched about twenty-five minutes before finding even a possibility of a place to drop our bombs so we could go home. The enemy was not primitive, and they didn't care much about this game, so they uncovered their radar searchlights and their antiaircraft weapons.

Suddenly our little peaceful black world wasn't so peaceful anymore. The first thing was being hit with searchlights that tracked every move we made. The aircraft was silhouetted on the clouds above us and the Fourth of July seemed to change dates. Caught in the light, we had to turn up the cockpit lights, try to escape the searchlights, and not get hit by the "bombs bursting in air" around us. By that time we figured we had done what we came for, aimed at one of the lights, "pickled" off (or released) the bombs, and hightailed it through the clouds toward home. After a short interval another *lucky* pilot had to enter the scene and start the next inning of this tiresome game, which lasted all night. Bad weather canceled those flights, and I prayed for bad weather.

We lost several of our classmates in Korea, not all of them to enemy fire. One crashed on takeoff. The pilot hit a crane parked close to the runway. Some had mechanical problems and could not reach friendly territory before bailing out.

Two pilots in our squadron made a mistake on a road reconnaissance flight along the front lines and bombed one of our own supply dumps, killing two of our troops. The pilots were quickly removed from the country, and the army general in charge of the dump was relieved of duty for failing to shoot them down.

TRADITION AND OLD METHUSELAH

Traditions are hard to break. Newly arrived pilots were called "new heads." Every other month the squadron commander held a have-a-drink-with-the-commander welcoming party. Everyone who had arrived since the last party was invited.

One tradition was a military benefit known as Mission Whiskey. We each were actually issued one bottle of whiskey per month while in combat. The government bought it under a contract with a Kentucky distiller. It had a black label and was called Old Methuselah. It was bourbon (or something close to that). I don't know what the specifications were, but the contracting officer must have been a teetotaler, because it was really bad stuff. In fact it was so bad no one ever asked for his ration, and the cases stacked up in the squadron supply room until there was no more room. Good drinks were inexpensive and readily available at the Officer's Club.

On the night of the newcomers' party, they brought out a case of Old Methuselah for the commander. He had a tent set up with folding tables but no chairs. This was definitely a stand-up affair. New heads would line up at the entrance to the tent and be invited to step in and meet the commander. Salutes were exchanged, names spoken, and handshakes were precursors to the drinks. The commander would then turn around and, from a selection of Old Methuselah bottles, pick one and pour two glasses, each half full. The glasses were from the mess hall and held about eight ounces each. Handing one to the new head, he would raise his glass to eye level, clink it against the other's glass, and drink it down in one gulp. The new head was expected to do the same and had been briefed to do so. The new head then left by the rear of the tent, and the next man would repeat the same ritual. All were supposed to leave the area afterward.

I didn't leave. I could not believe the commander could do that with so many men without passing out, and there were about twelve of us new heads! Finding a place where I could not be seen, I watched the tent to see what would happen. Sure enough, after each four men, the commander would duck his head under the side of the tent and throw up all of the whiskey. When it was all over, the commander went to the club and joined all of us as sober as a judge. I can't say the same for all the new heads. Naturally, they all wondered how he did it, but I knew. Maybe that's why no one ever asked for his ration of Old Methuselah. It was a macho thing.

KIM

Kim was a college graduate of the University of Seoul, and when the war came, he was displaced from most of his family, fleeing from the North Vietnamese with his wife and one child. He was given a job looking after one officers' barracks, coming to work early in the morning and leaving about dark every day. He and his family lived in a small hut in town.

Kim cleaned the building, shined our shoes, and did our laundry. At times he would also prepare soup and other dishes at the request of the guys. We ate all our meals in the mess hall, but snacks and other special things were always in demand.

As all Asian people do, Kim left his sandals at the doorway and walked barefooted inside. Some of the guys began to tease him by nailing his shoes to the floor or having a cup of water fall on his head when he returned to the barracks. Kim took all of this without complaining, the first time laughing with them. Repeats of the same tricks did not fare as well, and the jokers decided they were wrong in doing these things and apologized to Kim.

Kim smiled and said, "You no more nail shoe to floor?"

They said, "No."

Kim asked, "You no more pour water on head?"

They said, "No."

Kim beamed a broader smile and said, "Good, then me no more spit in soup!"

I always thought this story came from our barracks, but now I've seen it on the Internet a couple of times, so I'm not so sure. The lesson is a good one, no matter where it came from.

The hardest part of barracks life was packing up the belongings of a missing pilot. The lack of privacy was nothing compared to that. I'm glad they didn't leave the space vacant long, as a new head would move in within a day or so.

I added the fear of dying to my fears of flying and flak.

Carolyn

It is clear now that not being alone in the barracks was a good thing. That doesn't mean the same as not being lonely. Carolyn's letters were read and reread in my corner space. We had the "Achy Breaky Heart"[1] a long time before they wrote a song about it. Carolyn and I planned to marry immediately upon my return, and I dreamed about what that would be like. Her picture was just a shadow of her real beauty.

As my mission count grew higher, my time grew shorter. We were able to set a wedding date of August 12, 1953, as I planned to be home before then. I finished up my assignment, which, as it turned out, was just ten days before the war ended. By the time I received my new assignment and orders, they were using all the homebound flights to carry the prisoners of war home. Those who needed medical care were flown to Hawaii before going to the mainland. As soon as that was completed, I was on a plane to Hawaii and then home. Upon arrival in Hawaii we were bumped once more so the wounded could be flown back to the States. A week later I caught a flight to Amon Carter Field, between Dallas and Fort Worth, where Carolyn and my family waited for me. We had to reschedule the wedding for August 22.

God's second greatest gift to Carolyn and me is each other. Patterned after our relationship with Him is our relationship with each other. I have always known that Carolyn was a personal and very special gift from God. Maybe I haven't always acted that way, but that doesn't change my belief.

I first met Carolyn toward the end of my college days, when one of the many jobs I had was selling stainless steel cookware. Ivan Burgess, the district sales manager for Permanent Stainless Steel Cookware, hired several college students to help him cover the territory in West Texas. Andy Behrends, Jimmy Carter, and I were among them. (Not former president Jimmy Carter, but an old college friend of mine—a great dancer who owns a furniture store in Odessa, Texas.)

Ivan taught us how to prepare and serve a seven-course dinner in people's homes, as well as to make arrangements for and conduct sales presentations later to earn a commission. During the individual home-sales demonstrations, we would try to find another hostess for the next dinner party. Six to eight couples would attend the dinner and demonstration. No attempt to close a sale was made at the dinner. That was done in the home of each attendee. We paid for everything, used our own set of cookware, while the hostess provided dishes, flatware, glasses, and table settings. The menu was always the same: chuck roast, potatoes, carrots, onions, yams, cabbage, and baked apples for dessert. All ingredients were cooked without water on top of the stove. We always asked the hostess not to serve any alcoholic beverages, as they would diminish the taste buds.

Sets of cookware were not inexpensive for those days, ranging anywhere from $125 to $250 for a full set. We had to sell several sets to recover our costs and make any money. Ivan was excellent at closing these deals, and I worked hard to learn what made him so successful. He had an answer for every question and a response to every hesitation. If he couldn't get cash, he traded for something, usually of value, but sometimes not. He just did not want to come out empty-handed.

Late one evening while I was cleaning up and washing the dishes, Ivan came in to help me finish. He had the cutest young lady with him—his daughter Carolyn. She was sixteen. She smiled, picked up a dishtowel, and went to work.

I was so in awe, I said the dumbest thing, "Where have you been all this time?" It was the oldest line in the world. Thank goodness she didn't hit me with the pan she was drying. That triple-plied, highly polished skillet would have made quite an impression on my face. Instead she kept right on smiling and acted as if nothing was said.

When school was out I moved in with the Burgess family and slept with Bob, the next oldest sibling in the family. Carolyn's sister, Betty, was about nine years old, and Jerry was about twelve. It made our work together easier, as Ivan and I became close friends and worked many nights on the same dinner parties.

During the days we added a garage and another bedroom to their house. I helped Bob build a Soapbox Derby racer and did odd jobs to help pay for my keep. I kidded Ivan and his wife, Toppy, about making me work to pay for Carolyn, but they were most generous to me long before I asked for the hand of their daughter.

Ivan and I spent many hours on the road together talking about religion. I had been baptized when I was eleven in the Vickery Baptist Church. Now I was attending their church, Broadway Church of Christ, and enjoyed hearing the sermons preached by M. Norvell Young, who founded Lubbock Christian College and later became longtime president of Pepperdine University in Malibu, California. Carl Spain was the head of the Bible Chair at Texas Tech.

WEDDING BELLS

Four days after my return from Korea, Carolyn and I were married in Aunt Zelma Wilson's living room by Bill Bannister, from the Skillman Avenue Church of Christ in Dallas. Both of our immediate families attended. My Aunt Cora Osborn played the piano, and my brother-in-law, Frank Manning, was my best man. My sister, Frances Manning, was Carolyn's matron of honor. My mother, Rosa, wasn't too happy about my change of churches, but she attended services with us. She understood that most important was that Carolyn and I attend church as a couple.

We began our honeymoon in Fort Worth, and from there we drove to Galveston, then on to New Orleans before returning to Dallas. We packed up our gifts in a Lane cedar chest, shipped it to Yuma, Arizona, and left for the rest of our honeymoon. I had bought a new Ford Crown Victoria in Japan for stateside delivery, but Uncle Norman Wilson thought we could get a better deal, so I canceled the order and bought one in Dallas. It was light green with a black top. I had finished paying for Carolyn's ring while in Korea.

We drove through northern New Mexico, northern Arizona, and ended up at the Grand Canyon before heading for Yuma. Along the way we planned our budget. With flight pay I was making $450 a month. We figured we could save about $75 a month after meeting all our expenses. When reality set in, we were barely able to scrape by and we spent the last few days each month eating peanut butter sandwiches. We didn't mind. As the country singer Alan Jackson says, "We were livin' on love."[2]

ANOTHER AIR MEDAL FOR GOD

We drove into Yuma, Arizona, at five o'clock in the evening. The temperature was 117 degrees, and our car had no air conditioning. We rented a small house with some furniture and a "desert cooler" fan on one window. For those too young to know, a "desert cooler" is a metal box hooked up to a garden hose so water can drip through strawlike mesh. The fan sucks air through the wet mesh and blows into the house. The theory is that the evaporating water will cool the air. Cool, we learned, is a relative thing. Dropping the temperature from 117 degrees to 100 is "cooling." We eventually bought one that fit the front window of the car. It had a refillable water tank, but no fan. It only worked when the car was moving. At highway speeds, it was fairly efficient. In a sandstorm, it turned into mud. We always hit a sandstorm on our trips to and from Texas.

Not long after we arrived in Yuma, the air force renamed the Yuma Air Station base Vincent Air Force Base, which was the gunnery school for the Air Defense Command. When I arrived they were towing cloth targets a thousand feet behind a P-51, while pilots from all over the country shot their machine guns. I started off doing the same thing, only I was flying a T-33. It was a fairly simple procedure. They stretched a thousand-foot cable out on the runway, hooked one end to the plane and the other to an aluminum bar attached to a six-by-twenty-four-foot banner target, and off we went. We flew an east-west pattern over the desert, while the fighters flew a north-south firing attack on the target. Since this was a visual approach, there was little risk of shooting at our plane unless they fell too far behind. We had a drop zone for the targets and cables where they were collected, scored, and prepared for another mission.

Technology and weapons change. The Air Defense Command bases converted to F-89s and F-102s. They replaced the guns with rocket pods, and we went to B-45s and nine-by-forty-five-foot radar reflective targets. Huge tow reels were installed in the bomb bay to hold seven thousand feet of three-sixteenth-inch armored steel cable. The B-45 was the first mass-produced jet bomber. It had twin engines started by a five-pound canister of black gun powder and was operated by a crew of three. There was tandem seating for the pilots and a tail gunner's position, which was occupied by the tow reel operator. There was a place for a bombardier, but we didn't use it except for an occasional guest. The canopy was fixed and did not open except when we were ejecting from the aircraft.

What didn't change was the length of the runway and the temperature. The B-45 required more runway than we had when the temperature reached ninety-five degrees. If you landed after eleven o'clock in the morning, it was all you could do to get the aircraft to the parking area without having a heat stroke. Since all missions were finished by early afternoon, I arrived at the field about five o'clock in the morning and was flying at thirty thousand feet by daylight with my target a mile behind. We flew the same east-west pattern and north-south approach by the fighter. One time, however, the fighter pilot had his head in the cockpit staring at a radar scope and flight instruments, simulating night or an attack in bad weather. There was also a chase plane to make sure he didn't have us, instead of the target, on his radar lock. He usually fired one-half of the rockets the first time and the other half on the second run.

One beautiful morning it didn't work that way. A new pilot was on his first run, and he was excited. We knew he was excited because he had his thumb locked down on the radio transmit key, and we could hear him breathing. We even heard him call for clearance from the chase plane. What we didn't hear was the clearance from the chase pilot. And neither did the new pilot! He never removed his thumb, so he couldn't hear anything. He fired his rockets at us! They went all around us, but not one even scraped our plane. God earned another air medal.

The pilot, however, must have thought he had the devil by the tail for the tongue lashing he received from his commander. I never saw him and did not make an effort to find out who he was.

I added the fear of ignorance to my fears of dying, flying, and flak.

At the crack of dawn on another day we dropped the target out of the bomb bay at thirty thousand feet. The target fell down and back behind the aircraft. The tow reel operator had the brake on to hold it there while he made sure it was flying properly. This time the brake didn't hold, and the target started reeling out rapidly. The operator applied the brake but nothing happened. The target continued to unwind faster and faster until it reached such speed that the reel exploded in the bomb bay. The bomb bay doors closed as soon as the target dropped from the aircraft. The explosion shocked the whole aircraft, but we did not lose control, and there were no emergency lights on in the cockpit. I gently turned the plane around, and there was no smoke trailing the aircraft. We declared an emergency, I pulled the throttles back to idle, and we made a straight-in approach to the runway. There were no problems landing, so I taxied in and parked. A crowd of fifty or so was waiting for us. When I opened the bomb-bay doors, the shredded reel and a lot of the insides fell onto the ground, some parts even rolling several feet. It looked like a junkyard. The bomb bay was lined with hydraulic lines, fuel lines, electrical lines, and containers of fluids and oxygen. None were cut, broken, or leaking. Just one more air medal for God.

> **I added the fear of ignorance to my fears of dying, flying, and flak.**

Most of our leading jet flying aces were in the Air Defense Command and rotated through with their units. Major James Jabara, a "triple ace," was my squadron commander for a time. There were only fifty permanent officers on the base.

STAKING OUR CLAIM

About forty of us organized a mining company and set out to stake claims to as much of the desert as we could. Uranium was the modern metal of value at that time, and we thought we were all going to be rich. We bought Geiger counters, leather gloves, and rugged shoes. Then we headed out every weekend with all the water we could carry, a fistful of blank claim forms, and a sack full of empty Prince Albert Tobacco cans. We stepped off the claims and placed four-foot-high piles of rock on the corners and one in the middle. We put a completed claim form in the can and placed it inside the rocks near the top of the center pile. Later on, we took copies of all the claims and filed them in the Yuma County Courthouse.

We figured we had filed claims on more than two thousand acres when we discovered they were all inside the Yuma Test Station. The land already belonged to the government. (It's nice to know you were being protected by such brilliant military genius minds, isn't it?) Most of us will never work that hard again.

ROUGH DUTY

Yuma was actually a wonderful place to be, especially when young and newly married. Military folks quickly take you in and easily become your family. We all had ground jobs as well. I had about ten titles, including mortuary officer, personnel services officer, summary court martial defense counsel, Air Force Aid Society officer, personal affairs officer, palm-tree-planting project officer, and a few others that time has gracefully erased from my mind. We were in Yuma five and a half years, during which time so many significant things happened.

For every flying casualty, we had twice as many suicides. Sadly, we had more than our share of flying losses. My job was to arrange for the local mortuary to pick up the bodies of those who died and prepare them for burial. I visited the widows and took emergency funds to them as needed. Then I arranged for an escort officer to travel with the body to the place of burial. I escorted bodies myself several times to find out what it was like. Rough duty!

We had more than thirty casualties while I held that office, several of which were driving accidents.

Two officers involved in the same love triangle hung themselves. The second officer saw pictures of his friend hanging by his air force blue necktie in a bachelor officer quarters' closet, and he duplicated every aspect of it. It was a long and involved story.

The flight surgeon asked to be sent as an escort for one of the men killed in a plane crash, but he never returned from the burial in California. He left his deaf wife and five children to marry the dead man's widow. He was discharged from the service, and we never saw him again. We helped his family pack up and return to her parents' home.

I added my fear of disloyalty to my lengthening list.

It is often said that tragedies come in threes. I never could tell which three went together because we had so many. During an air show one day a Canadian Canberra plane made a wheels-and-flap-down slow flight over the crowd. When he pushed the throttles forward to recover, the right engine failed, the plane stalled, and we watched in horror as it crashed in the pond of our water treatment plant. He had two other people on board, who were just along for the ride. It took two days to drain the pond and recover the bodies.

Another pilot, flying over the desert, had to eject when his plane caught fire. We searched for hours before we found the plane, and many hours later and miles away we found the pilot. He had pulled his ripcord while he was inverted, and when the parachute opened, the shock peeled him out of the harness. He fell eighteen thousand feet. All parachutes were modified to prevent that from happening again.

The body of one of our sergeants was found along a canal where he had been fishing. His pickup was parked on the bank of the canal, about thirty feet above. It was untouched, and his keys were in the ignition. He lay face down in six inches of water with his feet on dry ground, fishing rod in hand. The autopsy showed water in his lungs, and drowning was the cause of death. There was no evidence of any foul play, and nothing seemed to be missing among his effects. Investigators surmised he must have fallen over from where he stood. The mystery was never solved.

A few of the suicides died by handgun. Several simply taped a garden hose to their tailpipe and ran it into the closed car with the engine running, causing death by inhaling carbon monoxide.

All of these people were on the same base with me. I wish I could tell you why they found life so bad while Carolyn and I were so happy there. It didn't make sense then, and it still doesn't. I guess I learned that you can deal with surreal situations as you deal with nightmares. You just wake up, smell the coffee, and get on with life. Also loving arms and a cold shower do wonderful things for the soul.

HELI ROUNDUP, DESERT BOB, AND HORSE POLO

While we were flying around the desert in the base helicopter, we spotted a herd of wild horses. The base commander liked to shoot rabbits from the back of the helicopter, and I went along to log some helicopter time.

We had already built stables at the base for recreational riding and had about twenty horses. A group of the guys decided it would be fun to round up all these strays in the desert and put them in our stables. Some of our civilian friends had horse trailers, so they joined in, and off they all went. I never did find out exactly how they did it, but they brought all the trailers back full of wild horses. I do know the base helicopter was a big help in scaring them into the blind canyon where they were roped and loaded.

"Desert Bob" was an air force deserter and fugitive. He had been assigned to a southern base and received orders to Thule, Greenland. Bob had an overpowering fear of the cold, so he failed to show up to catch the plane to Thule. Instead he caught a bus and rode cross-country to a drop-off stop not far from Yuma. He then packed up some gear and headed off into the desert. He would come down to the isolated store every so often, restock supplies, and the people at the grocery store would take him back out to a range of hills where he disappeared.

I really don't know how long he stayed there, but he had been away without leave (AWOL) for four months when he came to the base to turn himself in. I was appointed his defense counsel. With his help we located his

"Desert Bob" was an air force deserter and fugitive.

parents on the West Coast, and they came to see him. We never locked him up, and he had free range of the base. Bob was small for a grown man and looked older than his twenty-eight years, with his face weathered and tanned by the desert sun. I doubt there was an ounce of fat on him. His eyes sparkled when he talked, and he was easy to like.

One day he told me he would like to work at the stables. Since I was in charge as personnel services officer, that seemed fine to me. Bob was thrilled and actually moved into the tack room to live. I had other men assigned there, but they all stayed in their barracks and pulled shifts at the stables, which housed forty-five horses. Soon I began to hear stories about Bob. One day two of the men came into my office and asked for a private meeting. They told me they believed Bob could talk to the wild horses. They didn't want anyone to laugh at them, but they thought I ought to know.

Bob could do anything he wanted with any horse out there. They would follow him without a bridle or rope. They would turn in a circle or stay wherever he wanted them. They would let Bob put a saddle on them, and no one else had come close to doing that. I had already bought a goat at Bob's suggestion, because he said, "The horses won't get sick if there's a goat nearby." Bob's dad had told me that he thought Bob was a genius at math and had some autistic traits. He had always been a loner. He also said Bob had never been around horses in his life.

We kept putting off Bob's trial, as we all became attached to him. I talked it over with the judge advocate and the base commander. We decided to give him a general discharge and drop the charges. Bob's dad came and took him home, but we missed him very much. The wild horses were easy to break and became part of our regular riding staff. The goat was still there when I left. Bob filled my mind when I went to see the movie *The Horse Whisperer*.

Another interesting thing happened with the horses. We had a contract with the Goodyear plant in Phoenix for them to manufacture for us an inflatable, hard-rubber ball that was six feet in diameter. We filled it with a high-pressure air hose and played horse polo. The riders were not allowed to kick or touch the ball with their hands; it could only be moved by the horses pushing against it. Three horses and riders comprised each team. The goal was made by the horses pushing the ball against the fence at the end of the opponent's field.

We played in the riding arena, which was about eighty yards long and forty yards wide. The first games were short, as the ball punctured easily from the horses' metal harnesses. When we finally got everything wrapped well enough to protect the ball, a game might last up to thirty minutes.

At first the horses were afraid of the ball, but soon they seemed to really be getting into the game. I never saw this, but I was told that one day the troops put the ball and the horses in the arena without riders, and they played a pretty good game on their own. We were lucky none of us or the horses got hurt.

HARROWING EXPERIENCE

In those days neither the prosecution nor the defense required an attorney to conduct a summary court martial trial. There was an attorney who acted as law officer and made rulings for and against each side to conduct a legal and fair trial. We only tried the less serious cases, and the maximum penalty was six months in the base stockade. I defended thirty-two individuals and lost every case. I was able to get some reduced sentences, but I could never get a not-guilty verdict.

For one thing they never went to trial if there was even a chance the defendant was not guilty. If someone didn't show up for duty, it was pretty hard to prove he was there. If one didn't come back on time from leave, it was hard to prove otherwise. There were always many witnesses to everything. The best I could do was see that he got a fair trial and the lowest possible sentence. I never had one tell me he thought he didn't get treated fairly when it was over. We were allowed to use all the mitigating circumstances we could think of or find. In that context we became very inspired.

I was deep into the closing remarks of one case when they handed me a note that said, "Congratulations, mother and daughter doing fine." Carolyn had just given birth to our second child. Our first child, Jeff, was born twenty-two months earlier, and I was there for that one. At least they let me in the hospital. In those days you could not be in the birthing room when your child was delivered. Thankfully, that rule has been changed.

By this time Carolyn and I had some furniture and lived in a nice rental house on the east side of town close to the base. One day at work I got a call from someone at my house and was advised to come home as soon as possible. I jumped in the car and rushed home. Paula Frazier, one of our neighbors, met me with the news that Jeff had almost drowned, but Carolyn had revived him, and they were both at the hospital.

It doesn't rain much in Yuma, and our washing machine was kept outside on the back porch. Carolyn had a diaper pail with a metal lid, which was kept beside the washer. Jeff was about two years old and loved to climb on everything. He had climbed up on the pail to watch the clothes wash when he fell in. For some reason she can't remember, Carolyn went to look for him about that time and found him upside down in the washer with the dasher moving his legs back and forth. She pulled him out, screaming as loud as she could for help, and put him facedown on the kitchen floor. She started using the old-fashioned, life-saving technique of forcing the air and water out of his lungs. He was blue, she said, but when the water came out, he began to breathe, and color came back to his face. Somehow she had gotten the phone off the hook and dialed the operator, who could hear her screaming, so she sent a fire truck and ambulance. The manufacturers have since modified washing machines so they will not run with the lid open. This harrowing experience made the local newspapers.

Jeff had a black-and-blue bruise on his back and pneumonia from the soapy water, but after a week in the hospital we were able to bring him home in good condition. Surprisingly, he was never afraid of water as I thought he might be. During this adventurous time, Jeff also crawled up the refrigerator door until he reached the egg rack, which came loose, dropping him and the eggs all over the floor. Another time I found him walking on the top of the gas stove in his pajama-padded feet, trying to keep from getting burned by the pilot lights. How he survived childhood is still a mystery. He now has a boy of his own who is challenging him. I guess the Bible is right: "You reap what you sow" (Job 4:8, paraphrased).

Pain, Promotion, and Palms

For our daughter Suzanne's birth, Carolyn had a spinal block to ease the birth pains, and then she suffered tremendous back pains for days afterward. She was in bad pain when we brought Suzanne home, and we were just settled in when the phone rang. My father, Roy, had died, and I was needed at home.

Carolyn's first impulse was, "Let's pack the car and leave immediately." I knew, though, that she was under the effect of pain-killing drugs, because neither she nor Suzanne was in any condition for a twelve-hundred-mile drive. Instead I made arrangements for a military neighbor to stay with them, and I was able to get a friend to fly me to Dallas in a T-33. I was gone a week, emotionally torn between my loyalties to both very serious needs.

I called home several times a day to see how Carolyn, baby Suzanne, and little Jeff were doing and received assurances they were all right. About the fourth day Carolyn informed me the base had called, and my overdue promotion to captain had come through. She sounded good, so I finished what I had to do and returned to Yuma as soon as possible.

In and around Yuma were several large date palm orchards. One day we received a call from an owner of one of those orchards, offering us all his date palm trees if we would remove them from his land. These trees were twenty feet tall! The base commander accepted the offer and made me the project officer.

The motor pool issued me a flatbed trailer, truck, and driver. The Civil Engineering Department issued me a crane and a small dozer. Air Force Supply came through with fifty shovels, and I was assigned thirty to forty men each day to dig holes for the trees. We moved one hundred and fifty trees to the base over the next six weeks and had them planted and watered. Vincent AFB is now a marine air station, but you can see the palm trees from the highway, and they are still growing. It makes a fella proud.

Meanwhile I continued to fly the T-33, but I also checked out in the C-119 Flying Boxcar, the F-86D, and the C-47.

Hitchhiking To the Moon

We continued making lifelong friends at Yuma. Within two weeks of our arrival there, we moved to one of six furnished apartments on an estate not far from the Colorado River. All six couples were newly married and had much in common. There was a swimming pool behind the units, but a child had drowned there, and the owners had turned it into a giant gold-

James Irwin and his wife, Mary, became regulars in our social circle.

fish tank. Lily pads and frogs were in abundance, and the bottom of the pool was a slimy green.

We met one of the other tenants for the first time when we walked around to the pool, and he was up in the top of a date palm cutting dates from the tree—James Irwin. James and his wife, Mary, along with another couple, Kyle and Jojuan Redwine, became regulars in our social circle.

The First Hundred Missions

Mary complained to James that she had never hitchhiked. So one Friday afternoon James asked us to drive them out to the edge of town; they were going to hitchhike to Las Vegas. I had done this a lot while in college, so I had some idea of what they were considering. I strongly discouraged it, as I had been in one serious car accident and scared several times by people who picked me up. I couldn't talk them out of it, but James did say that if they were not back by dark on Sunday evening to call the Arizona Highway Patrol.

Mary was a beautiful young lady with long, black, straight hair—a Cher look-alike. James was about my size (5 feet 10 inches) and muscular, but not imposing. They had money for food and gambling but probably not more than a hundred fifty dollars. Each wore jeans and a T-shirt, and Mary carried a small handbag but no other luggage, watches, or rings.

Sunday evening I kept watching the driveway to our apartments for them to show up. Just as the sun touched the horizon, an old car loaded with kids and belching smoke chugged into sight. From somewhere in the backseat, James and Mary emerged, waving and thanking their benefactors. Mary's story was simple. They had waited for more than an hour before they were picked up and taken to Las Vegas. They spent every penny they had and were standing on the road back to Yuma when this car came along and offered them a ride. It was the same car that had taken them to Las Vegas on Friday. We prepared supper for them, and it all turned out well. How could we possibly have known that James Irwin would someday walk on the moon?

After he left the space program, he led several expeditions to the mountains in Turkey, searching for remnants of Noah's ark. Sadly, Jim died a few years ago.

THE PINK CONVERTIBLE

While we were in Montgomery, Alabama, for three months attending Squadron Officers School we traded the Ford Crown Victoria for a Mercury station wagon. A year or so later I saw a car in the showroom of the local Mercury dealer. After work I went by and stopped to take a look. It was a 1957 pink convertible with a black top and a four-inch-wide white stripe over each door. I traded our car for the pink convertible with all the bells and whistles. On each rear fender was a gold concave panel that began below the edge of the top and ran to the end of the fenders. It was "conservatively conspicuous."

If I should die the note on the car cut my net worth back to about five thousand dollars, but we loved being able to drive at night with the top down. We drove it back to Texas a couple of times, but it was not designed for dust storms. Taking the mattress from Jeff's bed, we made a pallet in the backseat for the children to sleep on while we drove all night on trips back and forth to Dallas, stopping for visits with Carolyn's family in Lubbock. After one particularly bad storm, we pulled into a filling station for gas and a rest stop. Jeff and Suzanne were covered with a layer of sand but managed to sleep through the whole thing. There were times when we had to pull over and drive five miles an hour due to poor visibility.

In the daytime the seats became so hot we couldn't sit on them. In early 1959 we drove the pink convertible to New York and shipped it to France, my next assignment. When it wasn't raining, we could drive around with the top down, and the French loved it. Every time we parked somewhere, we would come back to a crowd of onlookers, usually oohing and aahing. I thought they were jealous. Later on I learned that in French, those sounds were snickers!

3 South African Adventure

Air Force Logistics Command
Chateauroux, France
1959

Vincent AFB was phased out and the facility turned over to the marines in 1959 for a training base. I received orders to report to Air Force Logistics Command in Chateauroux, France. The military had all Carolyn's and my possessions packed and shipped, we closed our house and took a long leave on the drive to the airport in New Jersey.

My sister, Frances Manning, her husband, Frank, and their children, Mike, Patty, and Robbie, were living in Stamford, Connecticut. Frank worked for Mobil Oil in New York City. We visited them before turning the car in for shipment. Several years later the first North Sea drilling platform called "Condeep" was built in Norway with Frank as the on-site project manager.

This was a first flight for Carolyn, Jeff, and Suzanne. When we landed for a refueling stop in Newfoundland, Jeff and Suzanne also saw snow for the first time. We arrived in Paris with the two children and thirteen pieces of luggage. Somehow we corralled it all into a taxi and made it to the train station for the three-hour ride to the center of France and our base.

We were met by our assigned sponsors, who took us to the Hotel du

France in downtown Chateauroux. We had a large room with two beds, an armoire, a table, chairs, settee, bathtub, lavatory, and a bidét. The toilet, or "water closet," was down the hall. We lived there for two months waiting for our furniture and car. In order to bring Carolyn and the children with me, we had to have a pre-arranged place to live. Our sponsor had rented an apartment in a building about two blocks from the hotel. I rode to the base every day with a new friend until our car came.

In a few weeks I went to the port and picked up the car, the furniture was delivered to the apartment, and we set up housekeeping.

Jeff started school at a French public school. He was four at the time. The school called for a conference, and we thought they might not let him attend, because he didn't speak French. It turned out they didn't know how to teach him to write cursive left-handed! We told them all of our family was left-handed, and they allowed him to continue. It was partly true. My sister and my dad were left-handed. Our maid said Jeff spoke French fairly well, but he never did it around us. She was from Spain, so we really don't know how well he actually spoke French.

Meanwhile, I was checked out in three planes—the T-33, C-47, and L-9 Canadian Beaver. I was assigned to serve as the food service squadron commander and the personnel services officer.

French Friends and Pheasant

We met new friends, Bob and Jean Snow, in the apartment building where we lived. Bob was a high-ranking Civil Service civilian, and Jean was a talented woman of many skills and crafts. Bob and Jean introduced us to some of their French friends, who owned a chateau in the country. We had several dinners as a group and enjoyed them greatly.

One evening one of the French friends, Dr. Mossé, asked me if I had a shotgun. I said I did, and then he asked if I had ever shot pheasant.

"No," I replied, whereupon he invited me to come out the following Sunday afternoon to a hunt and dinner at his chateau. I had no idea that I was to be the guest of honor. A large wildflowered field stretched across twenty acres in front of the main house. There were thick woods all around the field, forming a U shape, with the house in the open space. The host introduced me to seven or eight of his neighbors who came to assist. I was then placed fifty yards in front of the house to wait while all the men went around to the far side of the woods and walked through to scare the birds into flight in my direction. One or two came up but were too far for a shot. We repeated the procedure all around the field, and I was able to shoot one nice hen. It was a thrilling event for me, not so much in shooting a pheasant, but the effort extended on my behalf.

We laid the hen by the back door and went in, neighbors and all, to a huge room where we had an abundance of drinks and gourmet food. They asked if Carolyn knew how to clean the hen, and she quickly said no, she had never done that before. In a mixture of French and English, she was given all the instructions for cleaning, preparation, cooking, and serving the bird. When we walked out the door on the way home, I reached down to pick up the pheasant, and it had miraculously changed from a hen to a large beautifully colored cock! The look on my face must have pleased them, as they all clapped and cheered. When we got to the pink Mercury, I asked the host if he would further honor me by giving the cock to one of the neighbors as a token of my appreciation. Carolyn breathed a sigh of relief when he graciously consented.

We returned to the chateau several times and loved to take Jeff and Suzanne with us. It seemed to be one of the most placid, pleasant, and peaceful places on this planet.

Carolyn and I were invited to a Reserve Officers Association dinner, where we met Hazel and Tom Bandler. Tom was the officer in charge of the base exchange, base laundry, and several other base service facilities, like the Class 6 store (alcohol) and the barber shops. Tom was the son of a New York lawyer and had inherited some money and property, but we never knew how much. Hazel was a vibrant, charming lady with real class. Both of them spoke French fluently. They lived in an area of Chateauroux, Balsan Parc, that had been a large family estate. The buildings and homes had been converted into apartments, and many military families lived there.

Hazel discovered that a new apartment was being opened up and made arrangements for us to see it. The estate still had a large functioning textile plant attached to the complex behind the building where the new apartment was located. They had made a living room out of the board room. It was huge, with a walk-in fireplace and beautiful wood paneling halfway up fourteen-foot walls. In the center of the room was a to-die-for chandelier. We took it on the spot and, with the help of friends, moved in. We lived there almost two years. We still use the fine wool blankets made in the mills behind our apartment, which sold in the United States under the trademark name Cabin Crafts.

We really became close friends with the Bandlers. Their son, Tommy, was the same age as Jeff, and they also became close friends. We traveled together over much of France on weekends, and when we moved to Seville, Spain, the four of us traveled to Madrid, Portugal, Gibraltar, and Tangiers. When we left Europe, we stayed with them in Washington, DC. They retired to Dallas and we kept up with each other for many years. In 1992 Tom had a serious stroke, and Hazel asked me if I would conduct his funeral if he died. Tom lived, but Hazel died a year later, and Tommy asked me to officiate at her funeral. Several years later when Tom died, I did conduct his funeral. We are still in touch with Tommy.

Tom wrote humorous articles for the base newspaper in a column he called *Tom Foolery*. When the base laundry burned, Tom announced in the paper how proud he was of the military people who used the laundry. He reported how "rich" most of them were. At least he assumed they were rich, because all the claims for lost clothing indicated that everyone wore expensive silk underwear, shorts, shirts, and dresses.

Tom was also a public speaker. In his opening remarks to the Transportation Council, he referenced how high-speed

> "**H**igh-speed . . . aircraft . . . made it possible to have breakfast in New York, lunch in Los Angeles, dinner in Hawaii, and baggage in Calcutta."

and long-range aircraft technology made it possible "to have breakfast in New York, lunch in Los Angeles, dinner in Hawaii, and baggage in Calcutta."

THE ADVENTURE BEGINS

The air attaché in Pretoria, South Africa, had flown his DC-47 (a C-47 with passenger seats, formerly known as a DC-3) to a repair-and-replace facility we operated in Berlin. We had loaned him one of our base's C-47s, in which to fly back home. When it came time for him to pick up his plane, he called our base and requested that it be delivered to him. It is a very long flight from France to South Africa in an old World War II vintage aircraft. Our operations officer agreed and selected a crew to go. I was one of the lucky ones. It was an involved and time-consuming task. Including an engineer to take care of the airplane along the way, a navigator, a copilot, instructor pilot, and spare pilot (in case of sickness), we were a crew of five.

We went to Paris for eight days, going from embassy to embassy to get passport clearances for all the countries over which we would fly. Most embassies required that we leave our passports and pick them up at the end of the day or several hours later. It was "tough duty" with all that free time to wander the streets of Paris. Carolyn, Jeff, and Suzanne went with me, and we did our best to see as much of Paris as we could. The hotel had babysitters, which allowed us to have some nightlife as well. When our task was completed, we went back to Chateauroux for what seemed like a million shots. We were flown to Berlin, where we picked up the airplane and flew it back to Chateauroux for loading. We had enough supplies, water, and food to last three months in the event we crashed in the desert or jungles. Finally, we left on our adventure.

We flew to Naples, Italy, refueled, and then flew to Athens, Greece. The air attaché had made arrangements at every stop for us to be met, taken through customs, transported to quarters, fed, entertained, and delivered back to our plane. Every embassy or air attaché along the route fulfilled that request in spades. We shopped at each stop and brought back a plane full of souvenirs, bananas on the stalk, and bottles of white lightening. I cautiously had the bottles checked for content when I returned, and when I found out what kind of alcohol it was, I used it to start wood fires in the huge fireplace. It burned with the prettiest flames!

Our next stop was Cairo, Egypt, for the night, then went up the Nile River to Khartoum, Sudan, where the Nile splits into two rivers. We stayed in the old Royale Hotel and ate boiled, cold carp with homemade mayonnaise. Then we made overnight stops in Kampala, Uganda, on the edge of Lake Victoria. Then it was on to Lusaka, Zambia, which is Northern Rhodesia today. From Lusaka we flew out of our way to circle and photograph Victoria Falls.

We landed in Johannesburg, South Africa, where we cleared customs and went on to Pretoria, our destination. We spent three days with the air attaché, having some work done on our return aircraft and getting some crew rest. We toured many native villages and listened to numerous briefings on African situations. This was in 1959, but even then they were forecasting most of the events that are still coming to pass in that part of the world.

We had planned from the beginning to circle Africa, and we stayed with the plan. The flight out of Pretoria took us over hundreds of miles of uncharted territory. We had the charts, but they were blank except for the grids. Most of the trip was without radio aids or navigational landmarks, such as rivers, mountains, or railroads. Our aviation maps for that area were blank, except for the earth's grid. We flew using time, direction, and distance, hoping to come out somewhere close to the seacoast town of Luanda, Angola. We managed to get the airplane down on the runway just as a rainstorm hit the field. We had been flying through the clouds for two hours and could see very little of the terrain around the area. When we woke up the next morning a ten-thousand-foot mountain was "guarding the city" from the Atlantic Ocean. It was beautiful but scary.

Our next stop was Douala in the French Cameroons. Accra, Ghana, took another day, and then we were on to Monrovia, Liberia. Somewhere back in our history, there had been an attempt to take slave families back to Africa. Monrovia is the port where they were dropped off. I was interested to see a small replica of the Arch de Triomphe with a banner that read, "Seek Ye First the Political Kingdom and All Things Shall Be added Unto You." I always wondered how that made all the local missionaries feel.

We continued to receive royal welcomes and all creature comforts from each American Embassy, even when we flew out to the Canary Islands for a three-day rest stop. From the Canaries, we went to Casa Blanca, Gibraltar, and finally back home to Chateauroux. We were gone twenty-one days and flew seven thousand miles. The last time I set out to circle a country, I ended up on a blacked-out runway. This time I made the whole trip. My per diem equaled my expenses, leaving me no poorer for the trip financially, but I had a lifetime experience I could never have bought at any travel agency.

France was alive with historic places, but military people have to make choices. The pay was adequate but never enough to splurge on anything (except pink Mercury convertibles). The choices were: (a) you could see the sights and travel; or (b) you could buy things like clocks, furniture, crystal, dishes, linens, and antiques. We traveled, and I'm glad now that we did. We thought we were going to be in France for four years, and we did put off a few trips, but not many. So when it came time to leave, we had no regrets about the things we left unseen. I saw my share of cathedrals and castles.

Want to see my slides?

4 Military Scam Exposed!

Casa Aeronautica S.A.
Seville, Spain
December 1960

Really good flying jobs are always hard to get in peacetime. Even then they are frequently attached to ground duties that require more time than the hours spent in the air. Since I had so much T-33 flying time, I was selected to fill an opening in a contract administration office we had in a Spanish aircraft company in Seville, Spain. They needed a test pilot.

In December 1960 Carolyn and I were packed up and sent on our way in the pink convertible. Jeff had a bad case of chicken pox, so we wrapped him in a blanket to cross the border from France into Spain. Fortunately, they checked our passports and waved us on through. Christmas came a day or so after we unpacked our things. A friend from Chateauroux was there and spent Christmas with us. We put a small tree on top of a table and decorated it.

Spain was just as attractive as France and seemed even more alive. It has a rich and illustrious history, and at the time we were there, it could not have been more exciting. My memories pale in comparison to those written by James A. Michener in his monumental book *Iberia,* which was reflective of the same period of time we were there. For all things Spanish, I strongly recommend it.

Seville is one of the most fascinating cities in the world. Untouched by WW II, tradition-bound, and secure in the hands of a benevolent dictator, the people were much as they had been for centuries. Modernism was just beginning to creep across the country, and there were two classes of people: rich and not rich, no middle class!

We enjoyed our new Spanish friends, Maria Luisa and Norberto del Barrio. Two other couples were also in our social group—Beverly and Joe T. Williams and Marge and Dave Davis. Joe was a veterinarian, and Dave was a warrant officer serving at Morone AFB outside of Seville. We all lived in a Spanish housing project called San Pablo that was very close to the civilian field where I worked. Casa Aeronautica S. A. was the formal name of the plant. And opposite page 330 of Michener's book is a full-page photograph of Salud Hidalgo and her daughter. She and her husband, Joaquin, were also very close friends of ours in Seville.

I fell in love with such Spanish favorites as flamenco dancing, *tapas*, bull fighting, *Semana Santa*, and *Feria*. *Tapas* are finger foods served before dinner, which was about nine o'clock. Each place was like a fast-food restaurant that served only one hors 'd oeuvre, with wine or bowls of olives, on the small tables where you stood to eat them.

Samana Santa is the beginning of Lent—a week of holy days when the churches for miles around mount their statues of Christ and/or the Madonna on floats that are carried in a parade on the shoulders of *stevedores* to the huge cathedral in downtown Seville. The women of the church cover the dress of Madonna or the cloths on Jesus with their personal jewelry. "Penitents," wearing tall, pointed white headdresses proceed the float, and men dressed as monks follow it.

The floats weigh as much as half a ton, so the men can carry them only forty or fifty yards at a time. These float bearers are hidden from view by a skirt on the float, but they raise it when they rest and are given wine to drink. It is quite a spectacle, and the crowds are huge. When they finally reach the "mother church," they go through the main entrance and the *Passada,* the statue is given a blessing, and they begin the arduous journey back home. The parade also features bands and other groups.

Feria is a celebratory fair with Mardi Gras implications, but it is in a fixed location like our state fairs. People come from all over the region and erect *casitas* (small houses). Daily parades of beautifully dressed women ride behind the men on horses. It goes on around the clock for a week!

Yes, indeed, Spain was a marvelous experience for us—one we will always treasure.

Test Pilot

Pilots from all over the European theater brought their T-33s to San Pablo for repair and reconditioning. The contractor kept the plane for a month or more, depending on how much work it required to be brought up to a new standard of condition and retrofit (modification). My task was to test fly each plane after it was finished, write up all the discrepancies found, and accept them back for the U. S. Air Force if I believed they met all contract requirements. This involved a thorough quality control (QC) physical inspection by a trained American inspector, plus my test flight. Doug Farnsworth was one of the best QC inspectors in the industry, and I didn't fly until he thought the planes were safe. Doug and his wife, Chip, were our next-door neighbors.

One of the maneuvers on the flight was to roll the aircraft until it was inverted, then push forward on the stick and hold it that way to see what would fall down on the canopy. We usually found all the loose screws and trash that way. My gratitude always came after I rolled back over, and everything still worked. In case it didn't, I finished every mission practicing with a simulated flame-out (SFO) landing. This is done by pulling the throttles to idle and gliding down to a touchdown on the runway.

> ## I found myself sliding down the runway on one main gear and the nose wheel.

One day I tried to stretch a glide too far and could not bring the throttles in fast enough to keep the plane from touching down before it reached the runway. There was a lip on the edge of the runway that caught the right landing gear and broke it off. Once again I found myself sliding down the runway on one main gear and the nose wheel. They jacked the plane up, put a dolly under the wing, and towed it in for repairs. My boss said he was glad I was not hurt and for me to go have lunch before my next flight *that afternoon.* "Hair of the dog" or something like that!

In 1961 I was sent back to the States for three months to attend the Air Force Contract Officers school at Wright-Patterson AFB near Dayton, Ohio. Carolyn was a little unhappy about that, as I was able to see my mother and Sid, her new husband, while there. But I also picked up another air force specialty, which was good.

Living in Spain in 1960–61 was almost too easy. We had a live-in maid for eighteen dollars a month and a yardman who also washed the pink Mercury. Carolyn had a hairdresser twice a week at home, a seamstress, and the local brewery delivered a case of beer for less than milk. The yardman brought the flowers with him and kept the yard in immaculate condition. One of our neighbors came by one evening to tell us that we were going to be required to pay social security on the maid. Sure enough, it was going to cost us thirty-five cents a month. The total monthly cost was less than thirty-two dollars a month for all of these services.

Those days are gone forever, and it is probably a good thing. The maid worked six days a week and went home on Saturday night. She always asked for an egg to take with her. We tried to get her to understand she didn't have to ask every week, but she always did. Honesty was highly revered.

We were in Spain during the Cuban Missile Crisis. Since we had no television, most of our information came over the radio or in the press. We missed some of the suspense and agony felt in the States. It was not believed to be as much of a showdown as it is now portrayed. Our Spanish friends had learned English from a former American consulate in Seville, so we had the ability to communicate well. The del Barrios owned furniture manufacturing plants in Seville, Barcelona, and Madrid. The general's wife from Chateauroux came down to buy furniture for the American Officer's Club in France. We met the del Barrios when we went to one of their stores looking for a source. Norberto offered to build samples for us to consider. We spent considerable time working on this project, and our friendship grew out of that.

The del Barrios introduced us to their friends Joaquin "Kinky" Hidalgo and his wife. Kinky owned a *bodega* in Jerez de la Frontera, and his wife owned an *aceituneria* outside of Seville. A *bodega* is an aging warehouse for sherry wines. The oak barrels in a bodega are much larger than the ones sold in front of the grocery stores. We had dinner one evening in Jerez and tasted two-hundred-year-old "mother" wines, which they use to create sherry wine that tastes the same every year. At that time Spain did not specialize in a vintage wine, where the wine tastes different each year. The Spanish devoted their efforts to producing wines that tasted the same every year, and the vintage (year) was not important.

Spain has a huge crop of olives each year. An *aceituneria* is an olive processing plant. They serve bowlfuls of olives much as we serve grapes. We had a dinner there as well. Both were white-tablecloth, lavishly decorated affairs with both waiters and waitresses, and a tour. Memorable!

Years later in Oklahoma when my military experiences, training, and adventures were reviewed for college credit, I was awarded two years of credit for foreign languages. The four years in France and Spain were, without a doubt, far more educational than twelve hours of classroom credit learning nouns and verbs. Carolyn and I have forgotten more French and Spanish than most students ever learn. We went to language classes in both countries but never became fluent in either of them, but we could get by well enough.

DETECTIVE DRAIN

My boss at the Spanish plant, Major Hinson, handed me a thick stack of papers one day, asking me to "check out these invoices." There was a cover sheet summarizing the transaction, requesting our approval and payment of ninety-eight thousand dollars for "local purchase" supplies. I sat down at my desk and began flipping the back-up pages listing all the items billed when one item caught my eye. It was for the flight suits I had received several weeks before, one of which was hanging on a rack behind my desk. I removed it from the hook, looked in the back of the collar, and found what I knew would be there—a label. Printed on the label was the nomenclature of the item, the size, the stock number, and most importantly, the U. S. Air Force contract number under which it was purchased. I stopped and thought, *Wait a minute. The air force bought this once, so why are we being billed again?* At that point, I really started checking the listed items.

I thought perhaps there was a logical explanation for this situation.

Military Scam Exposed!

The more I looked, the more doubts I had about the documents in my hands. I grabbed a cardboard box and headed for the company supply room. As I went through the list, I asked the clerk to show me one of each item I had selected for my test. I put them in the box, helped the clerk prepare a sign-out sheet, signed for the items, and went back to my office. My suspicions were confirmed! The air force already owned most of the items selected from contracts back in the States. Some of the items were just rubber gaskets cut from inner tubes, but the prices were astronomical. One or two parts might have been legitimate, but out of forty-five, that was not a good percentage.

I tossed the papers in the box and walked into Major Hinson's office, closing the door behind me. After I finished briefing him on my findings, he asked me what I wanted to do. I told him I didn't think we had much of a choice, but I wasn't sure how to proceed. Major Hinson suggested that I take my box, go into Seville, and visit the Office of Special Investigation. They would, he said, know how to handle this.

The special agent was a civilian, about forty-five years old and looked like Sean Connery (old 007 himself). He agreed that we needed to do something, and he would handle it. I was not required to do anything else and was never questioned again. We didn't pay the invoice.

It must have been much bigger than I thought, as the two American civilians working as technical representatives for the company were gone within a week. Two civilian supply workers in Sacramento, California, went to prison, and a general was relieved of his command. I heard that others also lost their jobs.

Shortly thereafter the plant received another contract, this time to modify F-102s. The contract had been at a French plant in Chateauroux. There was a test pilot already checked out in the F-102, and he had more overseas time left than I did, so he transferred in and took my place. I did get several rides in the F-102 before I left Spain. Nice plane. If there was any resentment toward me, the Spanish managers never showed it.

SAYING GOOD-BYE

It was about time to say good-bye to the pink Mercury convertible. In truth it was a real lemon mechanically, and with no parts or knowledgeable mechanics in either France or Spain, it became a source of more pain than gain. I sold it for four hundred dollars, but not before Joe Williams and I caught a flight to Germany to pick up my new Mercedes 220S at the factory. That was an experience! It took half a day for their chief engineer to describe in infinite detail how I was to spend the rest of my life looking after *their* car. Seriously, it was highly informative and made me really want the automobile when he finished. It had four doors, was shiny black outside, and had a rich, red, leatherlike vinyl on the inside. Joe and I drove through Switzerland and France to get back to Spain . . . in style!

5 A Matter of Survival

Brookley AFB
Mobile, Alabama
January 1963

We had the Mercedes a few months before loading it on a ship bound for New York. All our belongings were packed and sent to Brookley AFB in Mobile, Alabama, our next assignment in the Air Force Logistics Command. After our flight across the Atlantic, we caught a train in New York, and Frank met us at the train station in Stamford, Connecticut. Our car arrived within a week, and we picked it up at the port. After a stop in Washington, DC, we drove to Texas for a good visit with our families before reporting to Mobile.

If you have not seen Mobile in the springtime, you should. It helps if you have been out of the country for four years. There were approximately four thousand vacant houses in Mobile, as they had overbuilt, and the base was cutting down. We rented a new house in a nice neighborhood and enrolled the children in a nearby school.

On Suzanne's third or fourth day in class, the school called and requested her birth certificate. She was six on October 24, and that was too young for the Alabama school system. No amount of arguing or explaining that she was doing well in school in Spain had any effect. So she got to play until the following September when she started school in Enid, Oklahoma. It turned out for the best, as it made her a much stronger student for the rest of her education. She now has a master's degree in education and is a great second-grade teacher in Keller, Texas, a suburb of Fort Worth.

The air force tested my real mettle on this assignment. The Air Force Contract Officer School in Dayton nearly did me in, but in Mobile I was the division chief for 110 people, working to send out bids and receive contracts for more line items and spending more money than General Motors and Ford Motor Company combined. But there was a catch: they were all women. What a nightmare! They were so spoiled by their previous boss it was almost impossible to get the work done. There were massive abuses of sick leave, overtime, and personal problems even Drs. Ruth and Laura could not solve. Believe me they never covered any of this in school. I really believe I had things running smoothly by the time I left six months later. Some of the women were even beginning to respect me, and the swear word they had used in place of my name was being used less frequently.

At First, They Came for Others

The war in Vietnam was demanding an increased number of pilots, and instructor pilots were needed to turn them out. I was flying whatever aircraft the base had to keep up my flying time, and I had served their purpose in Mobile. That tour lasted six months. So we packed up again and moved to Vance AFB, near Enid, Oklahoma.

After getting the family settled, I left for Williams AFB near Phoenix, Arizona. A couple of months later I was a fully trained T-37 instructor pilot.

"This is an airplane," was the classic opening lecture when introducing a new student to the world of flying. From that simple statement to the receipt of silver wings twelve months later lies a whole new world.

These students were already officers and college graduates. They knew how to study; they knew how to apply themselves; and they knew how to work. Sponges, just sponges, one after another, absorbing any and everything as fast as we could dish it out. We were there to see that they did not get hurt or hurt someone else while learning. As I was told, they were the cream of the crop.

These students had six months of T-37s and six months of T-38s, half their days on the flight line and half in the classroom. It cost millions of dollars to train them. We could not turn them out fast enough, so the air force decided we could do it better if we had another airplane in the mix. Time was of the essence. Cessna could turn out their 172 models fast enough, and we could hire civilians to teach these young men to fly before we put them in jets. That required a civilian contractor, right?

Guess who had contractor experience? Yep, I was the only available rated officer on the base with that background. Two young second lieutenants (recent pilot graduates) were assigned to me, and we went to the Cessna plant in Wichita, Kansas, where their test pilots taught us to fly Cessna 172s. The air force version in production was called a T-41. We came back to Vance and wrote the manuals for the program.

We set up shop in the contractor's new facility at Woodring Field, the civilian airport, and made trip after trip to Wichita to ferry the planes down as they came off the assembly lines. By that time the contractor had hired some of the men who would become our instructors, and the lieutenants and I taught them how we wanted the students to be instructed. We were ready when the first group of sixty new college grads arrived. We trained sixty pilots every sixty days, giving each of them thirty hours of instruction. It was an easy transition into the T-37.

The civilians taught them, and we did the check rides. It was a beautiful operation. We washed out a few, but very few. We had a time limit, as we could invest only so many hours in each student. We had to decide whether to send them on for jet training or not. There were some tough decisions, but most of them met all the requirements, plus.

Fast-forward a moment. In the early 1990s, I was on a business trip to San Antonio, Texas. Just for old times' sake, I decided to stay in the guest quarters at Randolph AFB near San Antonio. After checking into my room, I went to the Officer's Club for dinner. There was a man sitting at a table alone, and I asked if he minded company. He stood, introduced himself, and offered me a chair. He had just ordered, so we talked and ate dinner for more than an hour, each of us telling our stories of how we came to be there and what our lives were like.

Finally, he said, "You don't remember me, do you?"

I looked at him, strained my mind, and said, " No, I'm afraid I don't. Are you sure you know me?"

He said, "Yes, I'm sure. You washed me out of pilot training back in 1966 at Vance Air Force Base." We talked for another hour, and it was interesting to learn that after he finished his tour in the air force, he took pilot lessons and had a civilian license. He did not seem bitter, disappointed, or angry with me. I suggested that from my experiences he might be alive today only because of that event. He agreed.

One of my lieutenants was later killed in Vietnam. Vance and Woodring went more than two years without a single fatality, and we graduated more than thirteen hundred pilots.

Mother Nature set us back one night when a tornado came through Woodring and destroyed seven of our airplanes. Each of the other training bases loaned us a plane until we could get replacements from the factory.

Most of the students we graduated went on to check out in aircraft that were involved in Vietnam. I saw one of my personal T-37 students in Guam in 1970. He was a B-52 aircraft commander.

Carolyn's sister, Betty, had lost her husband in 1965 to the war in Vietnam. She had a daughter by a previous husband and another child by the deceased husband, born after his death. The first child, Lisa, came to stay with us for a few weeks, and we offered to keep her while Betty tried to regain her life. Betty refused the offer. To be continued . . .

A Major Study

While I was teaching in the T-37, I did a study on air sickness. From that study I developed some different approaches to instructing. I became the "expert" on air sickness, and they sent all the bad cases of air sickness to me. I salvaged all of the airsick students but one. This young man had such a fear that he could not even look out the airplane window and count the treads in the tire below his window, much less tell me what he saw on the ground. He was miserable and we had to remove him from the program. In fact, I recommended that he be discharged from the air force. He would never have been able to *ride* in an airplane, much less *fly* one. He came by to thank me on his way home.

I was promoted to major from the work I did on that study. I had also just finished my college degree in night school at Oklahoma State University in Stillwater, Oklahoma.

And Then They Came for Me

The air force was looking for a helicopter pilot, and once again I had more time in a helicopter than anyone else. I protested vigorously because I was not primarily trained to fly helicopters, and they withdrew the assignment. Surprised, I thought I might have slipped by, but a few days later I had an F-4 assignment.

Please fast-forward with me again. During 2001 I read the Left Behind[1] series of books and participated in an Internet discussion group with other readers. In our exchanges, I revealed some of my history, but rather than rewrite this exchange, it seems more practical to just include it here, with the names changed for privacy sake. It captures what I have to say about several subjects.

Jenna: Jack, from your experiences in Vietnam, how do people respond under extreme interrogation? I know that in various armies, soldiers are trained to withstand interrogation, so that to the interrogator it sounds as if you are conceding or even giving away certain details that might be true. Sounds farfetched? My husband died in combat, and I know that they were trained for this type of interrogation. The exact details, however, were never explained to me.

Jack: Jenna, thank you for asking one of the toughest questions in the human relations field. Let me give you some details about my experiences, and I think you will appreciate my opinion, if not my knowledge, much better.

Before going to Korea and Vietnam, we were sent to "survival schools" to learn how to eject from an airplane and evade capture, but if caught, be a prisoner of war. It sounds like a terrible way to leave for combat. However, to go into harm's way with being captured as a distinct possibility and *not* be trained would be incomprehensible and totally unacceptable. The classes and physical training took twelve hours or more per day, seven days a week, and lasted four weeks. Some of that training is still classified, and I will not divulge any aspects that might give any enemy comfort or knowledge that could be used against our military people. E-mail is an unsecured medium.

A Matter of Survival

We were given extensive films and lectures descriptive of imprisoned political and military captives. They dealt with conditions that most of us could never have imagined: poor souls were kept alive year after year under torture by the most depraved men and women of this world. Some lived, and some died. The main theme was to find out why. Some were heroes and some were traitors.

What was truly significant, was the amount of distress and length of time the human body and mind can withstand crippling assaults. As they said in the movie *Jurassic Park*, "Life will find a way."[2] The most ennobling and enabling factors were faith, attitude, and perseverance. The first two can be learned; the latter goes to the innermost strengths of each individual and can and does vary greatly. Remember, survival is a natural human instinct.

There is a group that will accept any conduct (response) under imprisonment if it means "survival" (either life, improved physical treatment, or maintaining the status quo). It's the success of living-another-day philosophy or the ends justify the means.

In one such exercise we were kept up all day and spent most of the night crawling in the mud and rain for a mile under barbed wire to avoid capture. Those captured were taken back to the starting point to begin again. We completed the escape and evasion course only to be captured and taken to a realistic prison camp for three more sleepless days and nights. Our guards all had German accents, primarily because they were former guards in Germany, overseeing captured U.S. military men during WWII. Talk about *realism*! They were truly experts.

We were locked in single cells that were too small to stand in and not large enough, or we were not allowed, to lie down in. We were constantly being taken out for some different treatment or tactic designed to confuse and wear us down. One of the most frightening was a burlap sack put over our heads and pulled down below our waists and then being forced to crawl into a box just large enough to fit into by being in the fetal position. I heard others cry and panic, even though our minds told us, *This is only a training program.* Sleep deprivation alone, without harassment, can almost destroy a person's sense of reality. We were never touched physically, but there were individual challenges and group tests of our collective abilities.

> **S**leep deprivation alone, without harassment, can almost destroy a person's sense of reality.

After a day or so, we were all brought together and marched to a tented area where we were told that we were going to be given a physical "to see if any of us needed medical treatment or care."

As we entered the tent, we were requested to sign in on the medical evaluation ledger as evidence we were given wonderful treatment. We then visited with a "doctor." Several days later at our debriefing and critique on the conduct of the exercise, the ledger book was brought in and opened to the front of all our signatures. There, to our complete surprise, was a five-page confession and admission that we had all committed "war crimes" and renounced our allegiance to our own country for sending us to fight against the People's Republic, complete with irrefutable details of those "crimes." It was just another of the many tricks used against us to prove that things were not always what they seemed to be.

On another occasion, we were brought out and told that it was Sunday, and church services were to be conducted. They told us to form three groups to meet with the appropriate clergy. In one corner of the prison yard they wanted to place Catholics, in another corner, Protestants, and in an another, Jews. So we did as we were told. It turned out there were only three Jews, and the guards started harassing, taunting, and ridiculing them for their small number. In an instant and without saying a word, we quickly started changing places until all groups had the same number of prisoners. There was no church service.

We won one, and we lost one.

In my mind and in my opinion, there is little difference in the message between religious salvation, "to save one's soul," and secular capitulation, "to save one's life." Trickery and deceit are the devil's tools. Satan is the Great Liar. Followers of Christ must recognize that we may be slaughtered for His name's sake. After all, we serve a "suffering Savior." Standing tall and true to the cause, religious or secular, is perhaps the only weapon at our disposal. Death is the ultimate end of us all. What really matters is how we live, not how we die. Christ has promised we will not be tested beyond what we can bear. Any weakness or imperfection we may have does not weaken the power of God. Boldness in asserting our faith, without arrogance or ignorance, is encouraged by the Scriptures. In fact, I believe it is in our weaknesses that God will show His strength. To teach or take a position opposite to this is surrendering before the game even starts. It isn't in the attempt that we will fail; it is in resigning or accepting defeat as an appropriate reaction to the threat. In summary, it's all about *hope*.

So, Jenna, the depth and significance of your question has been studied for centuries and still attracts interest and conflicting opinions. The applications are as critical in our everyday lives as they are in these extremes of life-and-death consequences. It is truly a way of life! We are all "prisoners" of something or someone. I am a willing prisoner of Jesus Christ.

My last day in survival school was Thanksgiving Day 1966. When we unloaded from the bus that brought us from the last training event in the mountains, we headed straight for the mess hall. We looked like the walking dead. I passed an officer I knew at Vance, who had just arrived to start through what I had finished.

He looked at me in horror and said, "Jack? Is that you? How was it?"

With great relish and a forced smile, I answered, "Piece of cake, just a piece of cake; you'll love it!"

I turned and walked away quickly to hide my glee at the look on his face. At the mess hall we filled our trays with food, only to find out we were too tired to eat. I went to my room, showered for twenty minutes, and slept for twelve hours. I had lost seventeen pounds in survival school. I was in excellent physical condition.

George AFB
Victorville, California
Fall 1966

I then returned to Vance, packed up the family, and we drove to George AFB, near Victorville, California, for the F-4 check-out. We took our cat with us on the journey. Have you ever traveled with a cat? We learned we could not let the cat out along the way to go to the bathroom. At night the cat "went" in the bathtub. While we were driving, the cat was terrified and hid under the seats, scratching anyone who tried to pet her. When we opened the car door at George in front of the guest quarters, the cat flew out the door and ran under the barracks. We never saw her again.

We found a beautiful house to rent on Green Tree Golf Course in Victorville. For the next five months, it would be our home and that of most of our friends we ever knew. When anyone from another part of the country moves to California, you find out how many friends you have. They all come to see you. It was good for Carolyn, as she traipsed all over Southern California as a tour guide. The kids were in school, and I was at work. When Jeff and Suzy were available, they went along as well.

I will never forget the sensation of my first flight in an F-4. The incredible power and smoothness made me want to ride forever. The quality and technology made the F-84 seem like a horse and buggy. No wonder they still fly them today, forty years later. We did all the things we did at Luke AFB plus all the new Low Altitude Bombing System (LABS) maneuvers. In this delivery of a nuclear weapon, you release the bomb on the way up. The bomb comes off and travels to the target in a McDonald-type arch while you are headed the other direction to get away from the blast. With nuclear explosions large enough to cover the area of Chicago, you do not have to be as accurate. It is an old acrobatic maneuver called an "Immelmann."

> The sensation of my first flight in an F-4 . . . made me want to ride forever.

They let us do one flight just for fun. With an instructor in the back seat, we took off in a "clean" aircraft—no tanks, no pylons, and nothing attached to the outside of the plane. As we climbed out we headed for Death Valley. The F-4 really climbs when it is clean. At 50,000 feet I bent the throttles forward while diving to 30,000 feet at a 30-degree angle until I reached mach 2.2 (1,400 miles an hour) and pulled up to a 45-degree climb. At 76,000 feet we ran out of airspeed and fell 30,000 feet before we had enough air and speed to control the plane again. It was then necessary to head for the field and to land before we ran out of fuel. Believe me, they don't have that ride at Disney World! It was just an incredible sensation. In afterburner on a clean aircraft, you could climb straight up, since the available thrust exceeded the weight of the airplane. In fact as the fuel burned, the aircraft *accelerated* going straight up. All the new fighters do that now, but it was my first time to try it.

Capt. Richard "Red" Whitteker was assigned as my pilot in the back seat—my "guy in back" (GIB)—for the training. Our class consisted of thirty two-man crews. After my checkout, Red and I flew all our training missions together. Although already a captain, Red had very little flying time as a pilot. He had been a radar operator but was admitted to pilot training, graduating just before coming to George AFB. Carolyn and I became friends with his wife, Jan, as well. He brought an expertise in radar technology that I certainly did not have, and he was invaluable in the accomplishment of our training and missions in combat.

The training was stretched out, and I always wondered if the air force did not plan it that way. We had a lot of time with our families. I guess they knew that almost a third of us would not be back. It never occurred to me that I would make it and Red would not. It is hard for me to write about him.

SEA SURVIVAL

There was another difference in this class from the one at Luke. We had no accidents and damaged no airplanes. On one flight when we were having a dog fight with another plane, I accidentally pulled the throttles past the idle stop, shutting off both engines while in a heavy "G" maneuver. It really got quiet, and the engines were easily restarted, but it gave both of us a lump in our throats. Red never said a word. He knew I was embarrassed. In 5,000 hours of flying I never lost an engine during flight. Since most of that was single-engine time, it was an important factor in my survival.

A Matter of Survival

At the end of our training, we expected to leave immediately for Vietnam. There were no openings for us at that time. After several days we asked if we could go to the Sea Survival School in Homestead, Florida. The commander made a few calls, and we received orders for a class in two weeks. We packed up and went home to relatives. We found a house in Brownwood, Texas, about twenty miles from Carolyn's parents' farm, where she and the children were to stay while I went to Vietnam. I was insistent that she be close to relatives while I was gone. Carolyn had lived in Brownwood as a child and had many friends there. I flew to Homestead, and Carolyn drove down with Jeff and Suzanne to be there when I finished the school.

We attended classes, jumped out of helicopters in the ocean, floated around on rafts of different sizes, and had a ball. We parasailed off the deck of a specially designed ship, were drug through the water in parachute harnesses, and walked off hundred foot towers hooked to a cable, sliding down blindfolded to come up under a stretched-out parachute— all kinds of "fun in the sun." We learned to find a meal out of the rocks along the shore, eaten raw of course. The magic word was *survival*.

When Carolyn and the kids arrived, we drove to Key West, Florida, and back to Tampa to visit Marge and Warren Davis, our friends from Spain. With a major sunburn on my back from snorkeling in the Keys, we spent the next two weeks in Dallas awaiting orders. Next stop, Vietnam.

6 My Life on Loan

Danang Air Base
Danang, Vietnam
September 1967

For some reason I cannot explain, my mind focused on the men who fought in the Crusades as I looked out the window of the Pan Am 707 on the way to Vietnam. Even from 30,000 feet there was nothing but a few clouds and water—lots of water. Traveling to the sites of engagements and conflicts was not always this easy or luxurious. Thousands died reaching the wars against the infidels. Our troops faced grave dangers from German submarines crossing the Atlantic and Pacific in WW II. Yet here I was receiving the attention of flight attendants, eating decent food, and being curious about the future. "The times, they are a-changing"[1] goes the song. I had relative safety, comfort, and speed. What a difference life deals you according to when you are born.

The contract plane took us right into Danang, which from the air looked like a tropical paradise. However, from the ramp it looked like an American base under wartime conditions, only slightly improved from our Korean base at K-2. *Déjà vu.* A wave of remembered fears swept over me, and I could not stop it.

We checked in and were assigned to quarters. They had field-grade accommodations for majors and above, so Red and I could not be assigned to the same place. I had a small mobile home, and Red had a barracks like the one I had in Korea.

Jungle Survival

We had barely unpacked before we were shipped off to Clark AFB in the Philippines for jungle survival school! And I thought, *Oh boy, here we go again.* By this time we were really convinced they fully expected us to become POWs or shot down on our first mission. I became more adept at being a POW than a civilian.

This camp was run by Philippine Negritos, a pygmy race of jungle experts, who taught us the fundamentals of living in a tropical wilderness. The best thing about it was that it did not last long, and we were soon back at Clark AFB. Somewhere in all this Tarzan training I picked up a skin infection on my back, and I had to remain at Clark for a week of treatment. I was just well enough to play golf every day. Tough duty, but somebody had to do it!

Back to Vietnam and the F-4 combat check-out rules of engagement. Missions began immediately, and we finally got to do what we had spent nine months preparing to do. Coming back with bullet holes in our planes was common. Incoming rocket attacks were also common, but they were never a game to which we adjusted.

My brother-in-law, John P. Skoro Jr., had been killed in 1966 flying F-100s out of Phan Rang on an in-country mission. His wife, Betty, gave birth to John P. Skoro III in February after he was killed in September. He never got to see his son. John Junior had been in Vietnam two months when he was killed. We went to the burial ceremony at the Air Force Academy where he graduated. To be continued . . .

To say the atmosphere in Danang was intense is inadequate to describe the conditions. The enemy could have been as close as the Vietnamese lady who cleaned our quarters and washed our clothes. The enemy, without question, was never farther away than the perimeter of the base. Fear is more contagious than courage. Fear also lingers longer, gnawing away at whatever courage the mind creates. We learned to live with it.

Fast-forward with me again. Now that I am retired, I spend a considerable amount of time on the Internet. I exchange ideas and thoughts with hundreds of people. A member of one discussion group sent out the following plea for help in her arguments with some in the group who are quite clearly pacifists. The names have once again been changed for privacy sake.

Veterans Day
11 November 2001

Donna (not her real name) wrote this:

> As for what Christ wants for us? I do believe He wants us to protect ourselves and our families, and our country. These men [terrorists] are wrong, and they shall pay. In the Bible it tells us not to tolerate these things, that men should be punished. You cannot always turn the other cheek. Someone help me with these verses. Jack, Tommy. Ya'll know them?

My answer follows:

> Our dear Donna, I spent 21 years in the USAF, flew combat tours in Korea and Vietnam—two tours and 267 missions to be exact. I wrestled with this problem on many occasions as you can guess, being a Christian in the military. I was an instructor pilot for several years

and helped turn out more than 1,300 more pilots, who almost all went to combat assignments.

I lost many friends and former students. I even checked out my F-4 GIB before I left Vietnam so he could fly 25 more missions in the front seat. He was killed on his 105th mission. I bombed, strafed, napalmed, mined, rocketed, and flared bridges, villages, weapon storage sites, antiaircraft sites, railroads, highways, dams, power plants, water buffaloes, trucks, bicycles, trenches, troops, and many other targets I never saw on radar drops through the clouds. My students did the same things.

- Did we kill any of the enemy? Most certainly.
- Did we kill any of our own? Most certainly.
- Did I do all that in the name of Christianity?
- Did I do all that as a citizen of my country under the direction of my government?
- More importantly, did God allow it?
- None of my five children have had to do that!
- Do you know that Germany, Italy, Japan, South Korea, and even Vietnam have more freedoms today than ever before?
- Was that "the valley of the shadow of death"?
- Did it matter whether I lived or died? In either case God's grace would have covered me. *My life is not the most valuable thing I have.* Patrick Henry said, "Give me liberty or give me death." At the present time, we are losing our freedoms faster than I have ever known, primarily because of our own fears.

Most military people who live through a war feel guilty afterward for *not* being killed. We are haunted in varying degrees by that thought for all our days. We believe that the ones who died were better men than we were.

You want Scriptures? The Bible is full of war stories, overcoming evil men, even the absolute destruction of whole nations, who failed to understand and worship God. David fought with a slingshot. Some fought with a donkey's jawbone. Others fought with bows and arrows, boiling oil, spears, and so on. God fought with plagues, pestilence, fire, hail, locusts, and death. Jesus forecasted "wars and rumors of wars." God has seen fit to leave us here for two thousand years and maybe awhile longer without taking us away from evil men and an imperfect humanity. Remember, He is not wanting that any should die without salvation.

War is a terrible thing. President George W. Bush has said [about the war in Iraq] that we are after "evil men," but we are not after any religious group.² The men we are after are calling for a "holy war." I do not believe that we will rid the world of evil men, nor do I believe they will get their holy war. When this is over, there will be a lot of guilty and innocent people dead, wounded, and grieving. Maybe then there will be fewer evil men and a real holy war can begin—one where all the people of the earth work closely together to help the needy and serve God in doing the works He laid out for us to do. It is interesting that we crave and die for personal freedoms, while God calls for us to be *servants*, who "offer our bodies as living sacrifices" (Romans 12:1).

Attorney General John Ashcroft is quoted as having said, "Islam is a religion in which God requires you to send your son to die for him. Christianity is a faith in which God sent His Son to die for you."³

This remark, while controversial, is applicable to all those who, in the name if Islam, believe it is necessary to kill innocent noncombatants by suicidal attacks, such as bombings. It would help if Muslims who do not agree with these actions would *publicly condemn* the bombers and not just those who make the remark.

Could it be that Satan has muddled our minds? Will the truth really set us *all* free or *just those who believe?*

I have an engraved plaque on my wall that quotes John Stuart Mill, an English philosopher who lived from 1806–1873. It's interesting how relevant his comments are in today's environment, almost two hundred years later:

> War is an ugly thing, but it is not the ugliest of things; the decayed and degraded state of moral and patriotic feeling which thinks that nothing is worth war is much worse. A man who has nothing for which he is willing to fight; nothing he cares about more than his own personal safety is a miserable creature, who has no chance of being free, unless made and kept so by the exertions of better men than himself.[4]

Would I do it again? Yes.

How much easier it is to write such words on this side of the experience.

Silent Night, Holy Night

You may wonder why I believe God owns the medals I was awarded, and I only have them on loan. One of my friends said he believes God must have had many angels assigned to me, and they were all working overtime. I agree. God had a plan and purpose for me that included works I am still discovering at age seventy-nine. I wake up each morning in anticipation of what will be revealed. I feel the same way M. Norvel Young did shortly before he died when he said, "Every morning I stand on tiptoe and look over the horizon to see what God is going to do next."[5]

I published this on the Internet in 2001:

My Life on Loan

On This Night . . . Thirty-Four Years Ago, December 19, 1967

In the hills outside Danang Air Base, Vietnam. The United Services Organization (USO) Christmas program for military and civilian people who were very much aware they were a long way from home. A tradition, headlined by one of America's most famous comedians, Bob Hope. A makeshift stage, barely covered to shield the performers from the cold rain, mist, and light fog. Miss America, a famous movie star, and a cast of about twenty, including musicians, worked their hearts out to provide us with a few moments of relief from the fears and anxieties of our widely varied situations.

I don't remember all of the details now, and yet it seems just a short while ago. I was young, healthy, and alone in that crowd. Ponchos were the fashionable choice for the event. There were some seats, but mostly we stood for the entire show. I couldn't tell you one joke I heard that night, unless it was the one about how Danang got its name: it's the sound a rifle bullet makes when it careens off your helmet. It was a common joke but so much funnier when Bob Hope told it.

I was in Danang for only seven months, but it seemed like forever. During that time I flew 167 missions in F-4s. I had enough thrills to last me several lifetimes. The muddy hills where we were standing were frequently occupied by enemy soldiers who fired mortars into the base at night. Spent bullets often danced on the taxiways beside my Jeep when I was pulling supervisor of flying (SFO) duties. One hit an officer standing in the chow line ahead of me, wounding him in the arm.

Late one evening, from the Officer's Club, we watched helicopters pour machine-gun fire into a warehouse just outside the base where the enemy had infiltrated our network of guards. My roommate was shot down on the final approach to the runway. He ejected and landed in a riverbed. The rescue chopper took several hits while picking him up to bring him back to the base. It was that kind of terrifying excitement day in and day out. The field was never dark because of constant flares being dropped around the perimeter. One night mortar shells hit our flare depot. You could have read a newspaper for forty miles around the base. They hit our planes in the revetments, burning them into hulks of twisted and sickening sights. I lost 27 percent of the classmates I trained with at George AFB, California. Even my GIB was killed on his 105th mission, north of the Demilitarized Zone (DMZ).

The men and women standing around me that night came from all branches of our armed forces. I was older than most; I had been in Korea, but most of them had not. I knew all about the war. I had read all the books. I was halfway through my tour, while many of them would serve in Vietnam for a year or longer. We all laughed, howled at the pretty women, and forgot for a short span how very close we might be to becoming a casualty.

I was in the middle of the crowd, probably seventy-five yards from the stage, and as far as I could see in every direction from the reflecting lights were faces of every race. This show would end again, just as it had when I saw it in Korea in 1952, with the singing of "Silent Night, Holy Night." Have you ever heard 100,000 voices sing that song? I don't know what those men and women believed, but I do know that 87 percent of the 53,000 Vietnam casualties officially listed Christianity on their records. Have you ever seen a battle-toughened choir wearing ponchos and toting rifles?

We did pretty well on the first verse, and it was an awesome chorus.

The second verse began to be harder as we realized what was happening. By the end there wasn't a dry eye among us, and some unashamedly cried aloud. I still can't sing or listen to that song without tearing up.

I have often wondered where the enemy was that night. They must have heard us, even if they could not see us. There were no shots fired, and the peace that followed, as we all silently left the area, was overwhelming. My only conclusion is that we were vastly outnumbered, probably ten to one, by a heavenly host of angels.

My only conclusion
is that we were
vastly outnumbered,
probably ten to one,
by a heavenly host
of angels.

7 Back to the Front

Christmas Day 1967 I was on a plane to Hawaii. Carolyn flew to meet me the day after Christmas for a week of R & R. We did all the tourist stops and night spots. We saw Don Ho, Hilo Hattie and the cultural dances, went to a luau, and played in the surf on the north shore. We caught up on all our talking. I found out how she was holding up with the children and the college courses she was taking at Howard Payne University. It was truly a visit to paradise. She left on New Year's Eve, and I watched the fireworks from my room. I flew back to Danang on New Year's Day to complete the rest of my tour. My heart ached all the way back, but I wouldn't have missed a minute of it!

CROSSING SWORDS

My first act upon returning to Danang was to write an efficiency report (ER) on one of the pilots in my flight. Major Smitty Swords III was killed, along with his GIB, Murray Wortham, while I was in Hawaii. It was standard procedure to write the last ER and send it with his records. About three days later I received word that Col. Maloy, the wing commander, wanted to see me. I went in, saluted, and took the proffered chair. He said that he had on his desk the ER on Swords.

After a lengthy pause he said, "You wrote in there that 'Major Swords was killed on a particularly dangerous mission in southern Laos.'"

I said, "Yes sir, I did."

He replied, "You can't write that. We are not officially at war with Laos."

Stretching my neck out, I said, "That may be true, Colonel, but Major Swords gave his life on that mission, and I believe we owe it to him to record where he died. The North Vietnamese know we are bombing in Laos, the Laotians certainly know it, and we know it. It seems the only people we are keeping it a secret from are the folks back home."

Another long pause . . . "You will have to rewrite it, leaving that out," he said.

Now in deep trouble, I said, "I'm sorry, sir. I can't do that."

Then, to my surprise, he said, "I understand. I'll take it from here."

I stood, saluted, and left.

Officially, Maj. Swords was "missing in action" and remained so until the end of the war. I do not know if the colonel rewrote my ER or not. It was never mentioned again.

In a bizarre chain of events, I met Smitty Swords IV a few years ago, and we had a long lunch together. He has a son, Smitty Swords V. There is an F-4 (Serial No. 66-0368) on display at the Vietnam Memorial in Big Spring, Texas. The name stenciled under the front canopy is "Major Smitty Swords III." His wife never remarried and now lives in Lubbock, Texas. His family was told where he died but instructed not to tell.

Nonstop Missions

In March of 1968 our marine stronghold at Khe Sanh came under heavy attack by North Vietnamese forces. I did not think it was possible for the intensity at Danang to increase, but it did. We were flying missions as rapidly as humanly possible. The weather was below minimums at Khe Sanh most of the time, and we were making radar drops, one after another.

I was scheduled for the night shift during the heaviest part of the attacks. We took off about midnight, flew our radar drop, returned to the field, and taxied to the refueling area. Without shutting the engines off, we were simultaneously refueled, loaded with bombs, and serviced with oxygen. We violated every safety rule in the book to turn the airplanes around for our next mission. It was a surreal scene. I have never seen such a marvelous performance by ground crews, all working in the glare of flood lights, in perfect harmony and synchronization. It had all the attributes of a choreographed ballet, with authentic sound effects as music. Machines, weapons, men, technology, tempo, intensity, and terribly dangerous. It was one impressive sight!

We flew four consecutive missions like that, ending just after dawn. I understand the scene at the other end was equally dramatic and deadly. The C-130s were also on round-the-clock deliveries and hauling cargo out of Khe Sanh.

I also had supervisor of flying (SFO) duties during that period. I had a Jeep and toured the flight line as the on-scene director, expediting movements and resolving problems as they occurred. At the southeast corner of the field was a huge staging area for the C-130s. It was also where the Central Intelligence Agency (CIA) ran the Air America airline. There were four lines of C-130s. Watching them from the rear of the aircraft, I saw them unloading the dead into the mortuary trucks on the fourth line. The third line was unloading the wounded into ambulances, and the second line was unloading the POWs. The first line was loading the new Vietnamese troops being flown to Khe Sanh, all of whom were watching the other three lines. I could only imagine the fear that must have been racing through their minds as they waited to load for their turn to fight.

All of the POWs were dressed in black pajamalike uniforms, with black cotton sacks covering their heads and shoulders. They were marched single file, right hand on the shoulder of the man in front of them. About four hundred were being held in a sitting position on the ramp some fifty yards from the Air America terminal. As I drove over to get a closer look, something caught my eye in the middle of the outside row of prisoners. One of them had a light blue bag with his belongings in it, I supposed. Drawing closer I could read the printing on the bag. It said, "Pan Am." How ironic but terribly appropriate for the chaotic times.

At the Air America terminal was a tranquil scene, where people in civilian clothes were boarding an airliner, with Vietnamese women flight attendants in their native dress welcoming them.

Danang had parallel north-south runways. We were on the east side, and the marines operated their aircraft from the west side. The C-123s loaded Agent Orange and operated from the northwest corner of the field. The northeast corner, on our side, was occupied by the rescue helicopters and the Vietnamese air force. I was talking to one of the Vietnamese pilots and asked him how many missions he had flown.

"Fifteen hundred," he replied.

I thought, *Good grief, and I thought I had it tough! This poor fellow has to fly combat missions until he is killed, wounded, or the war ends.*

This Little Light of Mine

Not everything we did as soldiers was destructive or unrewarding, though. Opportunities were everywhere to help the hurting, those whose lives had been destroyed, those in pain. We had many chances to shine the light of Christ into that dark and dismal world.

For instance, there was a Church of Christ orphanage in the city of Danang. Several of us went there to help and took all the food and supplies we could scrounge. As in the Korean War, there are always many children who have lost their parents.

I asked Carolyn to get her sorority in Brownwood, Texas, to send clothing. They sent us several large containers of children's clothes. The Vietnamese are small people and could not wear any of our adult sizes. I also attended church services on the base with a small group of church members.

These activities refreshed my soul and kept me going when the world seemed to be blowing up all around me.

Golden

A combat pilot has a silent and secret enemy. I can only trace its origin to the remark I made the day we became pilots. This may even be a backlash to the motivational technique of constantly telling us in training that we were the *cream of the crop*. In combat that phrase changes to one word, *golden*. After so many missions, pilots begin to believe they cannot be killed. The exact number of missions varies from pilot to pilot.

After so many missions, pilots begin to believe they cannot be killed.

Most of us did not recognize this subtle enemy until we did something that, in retrospect, was unwise. We pressed a target, made an unnecessary extra pass, pushed the aircraft to the edge of its limitations or beyond. Maybe we flew a mission when physically less than our best for whatever reason. I was able to spot golden in others before I found it in myself. It was all too often a deadly enemy. Golden, stripped of its glitter, is simply arrogance and ignorance.

Climbing into the Front Seat

Whenever possible, Red flew from the backseat. He had even landed the aircraft from that position. He was a cool hand on the controls' flying formation, and I knew it was eating him alive to get a chance at the front seat. When the opportunity came, Red jumped at the chance to upgrade. The wing commander authorized us to train six volunteers to fly in the front seat, and Red was one of them. However, there was a catch as each man had to extend his tour and fly twenty-five more missions up north. I did not think it was worth it and tried to talk Red out of doing it, but he was committed.

So I flew in the backseat for my last fifteen north missions and several in-country missions checking Red out. He was like a sponge, soaking up everything as fast as I could dish it out. I was back in the States checking out in the KC-135 when I learned that Red had been killed on his 105th north mission. Jim Badley, riding in the backseat, was also killed. I was heartsick and felt so guilty that I could not talk Red out of staying.

The report I received indicated that he had simply flown into the target. My brother-in-law had done the same thing in his F-100. I am still not convinced that is all of the story. Both Red and Jim knew what the minimum roll-in altitudes were. They also knew the minimum altitudes for recovery to stay above the ground fire. I do know, however, the temptation to press an attack to accomplish a mission. We will never know all the answers to our questions.

A much older man smiled at the flight attendant on the chartered 707 as the plane lifted off for the flight home to Carolyn and the children. I did not spend much time thinking about how men from the Crusades or other wars returned home.

A plaque on my wall was given to me when Red and I celebrated our 100th mission. The following list is from signatures on that plaque and is the best deciphering my old eyes will do with a magnifying glass. If some are misidentified, I sincerely apologize. I include them on the following page to honor their service and sacrifice to America.

Survivors of the Short-Fuse Bombs
Who Signed Jack's Squadron Plaque

John E. Allen	N. A. Kruk
Andy Anderson	Bert R. Langford
Al Audette	Bob Lea
Jim Badley	Charles E. Lewis
Bob Barrett	T. McGourin
Chuck Beaver	Jack Marlieus(?)
George Bivens	C. H. Meier
David P. Brewer	Jay A. Milstead
Philip L. Brewster	Clint Moses
Bob Brockman	Duke Mouland
N. J. Brower	Glenn L. Nordin
Les Brown	Bill Palmer
Larry Busete	Dave Pennington
Tom Casper	Donald W. Pick
Clasen P. Conway	John L. Pickett
George Dolan	Marlin C. Richard
Hank Dolim	Bob Riddick
Joe Fitzgerald	Al Rodriguez
John B. Flagg	Carly Savelle
Sam Graves	Skip Scott
Rex Hammack	Bobby Shannon
J. P. de la Hanssage	Les Spencer
Dennis M. Harper	Mike Stevens
Chuck Hendrix	David Stokes
Edward Huekner	J. W. Stone
Mark Jensen	Nathan H. Thomas
Harry John	Billy Vasser
Jerry Johnston	Paul C. Watson
Gordon Jones	Richard P. Whittaker
Joseph P. Kosciusko	Norm Wilson

8 Strategic Air Command

Castle AFB
Atwater, California
April/May 1969

After a wonderful reunion with my family, I left to attend a KC-135 training school at Castle AFB near Atwater, California. In Enid I was flying the lightest airplane, in Vietnam I was flying one of the fastest airplanes, and now I was going to fly one of the heaviest planes in the U. S. Air Force. All of this was within a two-year period. After being a loner at the controls, I had to learn to fly with a group or team, but I was just happy to be flying anything that wasn't a target!

I had this assignment at the half-way point in Vietnam. I had requested Oklahoma City or San Antonio, so they put me in between in Fort Worth, Texas. I had no idea what a tour in the Strategic Air Command (SAC) would be like. When Carolyn and the kids finished the school year in Brownwood, they joined me in California, so this time we got to see the northern part of the state.

On the way back to Texas, we drove through Yuma, Arizona, to let the kids see where they were born. We found the county hospital, and as we drove by, Jeff read the sign: "Edna Gladney Home for Unwed Mothers."

We should have called ahead! The county hospital where they were born had been converted into the Edna Gladney Home.

In eighteen years of military service, we had never bought a house. We either rented one, or it was provided by the military. Peggy and Jim Davis, friends from our Enid days, helped us buy the right home in Hurst, Texas, for our assignment at Carswell AFB near Fort Worth. The number one consideration for us was the school district. The house was a new, four-bedroom on the edge of a growing city. Coming events were going to require every inch of space in that house.

A Difficult Time

We had barely unpacked when Carolyn's mother called from Lubbock. Carolyn's sister, Betty, and her two children had gone to Tucson, Arizona, to be with a lieutenant she had met while he was in pilot training at Reece AFB. The lieutenant had called, scared to death: He said, "Betty is holed up in a motel with the children, and she is out of her mind." We had received reports of her problems all the time I was in Vietnam.

The lieutenant was going through the GIB program and on his way to Vietnam. I took emergency leave, called the lieutenant's squadron commander and asked him to allow the lieutenant to drive us all to Lubbock. Betty's brother, Jerry, was to make arrangements for us to put Betty in the Methodist hospital in Lubbock.

I caught a commercial flight to Tucson, was met by the lieutenant, and we went to get Betty. The flight surgeon at Davis-Monthan AFB had given me some tranquillizers, and we were able to get Betty to take one. We loaded all her things and drove straight through to Lubbock, keeping Betty asleep in the backseat with the tranquilizers. With the doctor's help in Lubbock, the judge committed Betty to treatment and made Carolyn and me temporary guardians for Betty and the children. I brought Lisa, age five, and John, age two, home with me. We didn't have a clue about what was going to happen. We just did what we knew to do for each day. I heard later that the lieutenant was killed in Vietnam.

About a month later we received a phone call from the hospital asking us to come get Betty. They were "through," and she was ready to be taken home. I thought they meant they had *fixed* whatever was wrong, and she was able to resume her life. I drove to Lubbock and went to the hospital. Betty didn't know who I was! She had been given twenty-three electric-shock treatments and was as happy as a clam. She didn't know who she was either.

By the time we reached home in Hurst, I was scared. We set Betty up in a private bedroom, gave her a phone and began the slow, arduous task of bringing her back to reality. We had never heard of paranoid-schizophrenia and certainly didn't have a clue, or any instructions from the doctors, about how to treat her. (We recently saw the movie *A Beautiful Mind*, which had a distinctly different meaning to us than to the general audiences.)

The next six months were the worst

We had never heard of paranoid-schizophrenia and certainly didn't have a clue, or any instructions from the doctors, about how to treat her.

days of our lives. I was pulling alert at the base seven days and seven nights, while Carolyn had four children and her sister to corral. We talked a lot on the phone, but I could not leave the base, and things were not going well at home. Betty ran up a $350 long distance phone bill, calling everyone in our address book, asking, "Do you know me?" By the time the shocks wore off in six months, Betty was worse than before. We had to have her committed to Timberlawn Hospital on the east side of Dallas with the understanding that we would be made aware of all her treatments.

We received weekly written reports and went to see her every week. After three months, the doctors called us in for a consultation and informed us, "If Betty had cancer, we would tell you we cannot operate." In other words, they struck out. Shortly after she came back to our house, she decided to go to Lubbock. We did not try to stop her, but we did keep the children with us.

I then knew, in part, why God let me live through Korea and Vietnam. He needed Carolyn and me to rear the children from that time on. The court granted us permanent guardianship of all three, but only the children lived with us. Betty became a nomad, refusing to live close to any of her family. She was in and out of five more hospitals for treatment but never found her place in life. We could write another whole book on our experiences with her during this period.

Betty died at age forty-eight in a mobile home in Amarillo, Texas, and was taken to the hospital as "Jane Doe." One of her friends remembered that Betty received monthly checks from Western Union, and they traced us down to let us know she had died. Betty had been dead for a week when we received the call. Her friend only knew her as "Lulu." She carried no identification.

Betty's body was brought back to Lubbock for burial. Her father, Ivan, had died in 1970, but her mother, Coye, sister Carolyn, brothers Bob and Jerry, children Lisa and John, and other members of the family held a graveside service. We celebrated her sweet life before the tragedy of her husband's death had changed her life forever. She is buried next to her father and grandparents. It was the first time I ever saw funeral home attendants openly cry.

Betty's problems are not uncommon in our society, which has to deal with those unfortunate conditions. The medical field has very few answers and for an understandable reason. Every one of the paranoid-schizophrenics is unique enough to require specific treatment. It seems to hinge on the patient's willingness to recognize and accept the need for help. Betty was unable to do that. There may have been medications that would have changed her life, but she was unwilling and, in my opinion, unable to allow herself to be medicated. It was a part of her illness. She became extremely "street smart" when in the forced custody of psychiatrists and able to manipulate them in a short period. Betty was mentally alert and had the ability to learn, but her personal fears overwhelmed her. In some ways she believed she was the normal one and we were all sick. She was, in many ways, a victim of the Vietnam War.

Rearing her children has been such a blessing to us.

ANGELS ON OUR WINGS

As an aircraft commander in SAC, our mission, in case of war, was to scramble the KC-135, refuel a B-52 over Canada, and hope we could find a place to land before flaming out. We were to give all the fuel to the bomber it could take, even if we had none left. A KC-135 (military version of the Boeing 707) weighs 100,000 pounds empty. Fully loaded with fuel, it weighs more than 300,000 pounds. It is one heavy dude. The plane also does not perform well at that weight. Carswell has a 12,000-foot runway, and it takes all of it to get airborne at that weight. Being on alert every other week would not have been so bad, if my family had not been enduring such stressful times.

Frequently SAC practiced a full-scramble alarm. The crews on alert would rush to our airplane, start the engines, and taxi out to the end of the runway before canceling the mission. One mission was not canceled, and we attempted to take off. About halfway down the runway we did not have the proper speed at the go-no-go decision point. I had to cut the power and try to stop the plane before it went off the end of the runway. We had seen training films on max weight take-offs and aborted stops. In the films the aircraft brakes became so hot they burst into flames. We barely got the aircraft slowed down enough to turn off the runway and stop. We quickly evacuated the plane and ran away as fast as we could. The fire trucks arrived and foamed the wheels before they could burn.

Again the angels sang while pushing back on the wings.

The end of that runway is only about half a mile away from a Neiman Marcus store in a mall. An explosion of 200,000 pounds of fuel would have lit up the neighborhood. Again the angels sang while pushing back on the wings.

My crew and I took two trips during the year we spent on alert. On the first one we took off from Fort Worth and landed in Madrid, Spain. If needed we had enough fuel left to make it to Istanbul, Turkey. We were in Spain a month, flying missions from the Arctic Sea to Italy and over the Atlantic as far as the Azores. We air-refueled a wide variety of planes during those missions. The one near the Azores was a night refueling of a B-52 between thunderstorms. On our return flight from Spain, we left Madrid, picked up a flight of four F-4s over England, nursed them to Detroit, and landed in Fort Worth.

On the second trip we flew to Hawaii, refueled, and landed in Guam. The KC-135 has access to all the fuel it can carry, which gives it tremendous range if it does not refuel other aircraft. We never carried a spare crew member, so our "low energy factor" was more of a limitation than the plane's fuel.

A plaque on my wall is titled "KC-135 Crew of the Quarter, February 1969." I remember it was not long after we won that award when I became Carswell's Organizational Maintenance Squadron Commander (OMS). My work days dropped from twenty-four to twelve hours a day. And weekends off! This lasted for five months before the wing (usually made up of three squadrons) deployed for six months on an Arc-Lite assignment to the Far East. Arc-Lite was the name of the SAC program rotating all their Wings to and from the war area in the Far East in support of the war in Vietnam. All of our KC-135 tankers and B-52 bombers joined the fight in Vietnam.

My squadron at Carswell maintained both types of aircraft, but I never went inside a B-52 until I found myself the maintenance officer at Guam for forty-two combat-flying B-52s. A month before we arrived in Guam, a B-52 had lost the right wing immediately after take-off, scattering a full load of bombs and crew over the ocean above the Marianas Trench—the deepest ocean floor in the world. I was determined that was not going to happen on my watch. I may not have contributed much else, but I personally inspected the main wing spars of every aircraft before every mission.

After three months I was transferred to Okinawa, where I became the night deputy commander for maintenance with a squadron of B-52s and a squadron of KC-135s. I flew missions into Vietnam in the B-52 and the KC-135.

While I was in Okinawa, one of our KC-135s crashed off the coast of Taiwan shortly after take-off. I was a member of the accident investigation board, spending three weeks in Taipei, Taiwan (Formosa).

We concluded that the tail had come off, but we did not recover enough of the plane to be absolutely certain of our decision. There were no radio transmissions or survivors. Most of the wreckage found was charred, but that most likely occurred when the plane burst into flames on impact.

FAMILY MATTERS

Carolyn was pregnant when I left for this adventure. David was born two weeks after my return from Asia. Until the birth of David, we had two families—our own children and Betty's children. David's birth united us, as he was everyone's little brother. Suzanne claims she raised David, but he was closer to John's age than the others, so they easily became friends. David and John attended Abilene Christian University (ACU), sharing one year of college—when John was a senior, David was a freshman. John played varsity football for his four years, while David was a cheerleader for his four years. Our oldest son, Jeff, had attended ACU one year and played in the "Big Purple" band. Suzanne graduated from there and received her master's degree from Texas Woman's University in Denton, Texas. We kept the highway between Fort Worth and Abilene hot for many years. It was wonderful to watch one play in the band, one play in the football game, while being led in the cheers by another of our children. Carolyn and I were happy!

A FOND FAREWELL

I was the assistant director of maintenance when we returned from Arc-Lite. I was promoted to lieutenant colonel, spending my last six months on active duty as the wing executive officer. This was considered a "cushy" job, to give me time to prepare for retirement. I drafted all the commander's efficiency reports, wrote his letters to the troops in the base newspaper, and prepared speeches he delivered around Fort Worth.

My last flight for pay was in a C-47. I had not missed a month of flight pay since I began pilot training. Retirement came after twenty-one years, a chest full of ribbons, and enough thrills to last several lifetimes. I had logged 5,000 hours of flying time in 24 different aircraft, visited 37 states and 24 foreign countries. And I came out alive and well. God was so good to me.

I had logged
5,000 hours of
flying time in 24
different
aircraft,
visited 37 states
and 24 foreign
countries. And I
came out alive and
well. God was so
good to me.

9 Unanswered Questions

Carswell AFB
Fort Worth, Texas
1970-71

During my time at Carswell AFB, I worked some on a master's degree. One course taught by an elderly gentleman stood out to me more than others because it had a strong influence on my thinking. It focused on "the *heuristic* question." Don't worry if you have never heard that word before; few of us had. The heuristic question concerns the art and skill of being able to ask a question that is equally balanced. It is speaking on level terms to people of any age, any level of competence, without prejudicially influencing the response. It is when you do not talk up or down to anyone. It is made up of body language, facial expression, tone, and volume of voice. If the format is in written communication, it is style, selection of words, punctuation, grammar, spelling, structure, and circumstances. The dictionary defines *heuristic* as "a way to solve problems for which no theory or formula exists." An example would be the process of trial and error.

I understand the concept, but the practice sometimes eludes me. When I am on track, people respond by telling me more than I want to know. When I forget the rules, people shut me out or end the conversation prematurely. All of us can recall situations we handled badly.

You're probably wondering, what does the heuristic question have to do with the purpose of this book? If you asked yourself, "How would I have handled that?" you are on the way to answering the question. To help out even more, read the following stories and ask, "What would I have done about that?"

A TRILOGY OF CONSEQUENCES

Earlier I mentioned that we had to fly missions to dispose of the vast amount of war supplies being unloaded at the docks in Vietnam. Here's a trilogy of consequences:

Willie Petes and buffaloes. On missions where weather permitted, specific targets were marked for us by a forward air controller (FAC). The FAC would direct us to the area and mark the target with a white phosphorous rocket called a "Willie Pete." As each aircraft attacked, the FAC would issue new directions and instructions from the bomb blasts of each plane. When we had expended all ordnance, the FAC searched the area and reported bomb damage assessments (BDAs) for us to pass on to Air Force Intelligence during our mission debriefings. We were usually given credit for so many feet of trenches destroyed, cuts in roadways, the number of those killed in action (KIA), number of antiaircraft guns, tanks, trucks, and the like destroyed. FACs flew in light aircraft and were subject to ground fire on every flight. They must have been the bravest among us to do their jobs so well.

On one mission into southern Laos (1968), the FAC led us to a lake and informed us there were six water buffaloes standing in the lake.

As pilot of the lead aircraft, I acknowledged his information and asked, "Okay, what is the target?"

"The water buffaloes," he said.

"Are you serious?" I asked, again thinking he must have something else in mind.

"Yes, they use them as pack animals to haul supplies."

"Have you seen any enemy activity in this area, any weapons or ground fire?"

"No, but that is all I have for you."

So we set up a pattern, dropped one bomb at a time from each plane until we used everything we had. There was no resistance. As we left the target area, the FAC notified us we could claim "six animal trucks" as our BDA.

The more I thought about the mission, the sicker at heart I became. We had used two expensive F-4s, more than $40,000 of ordnance, full loads of fuel, and worse, risked the lives of four crewman and the FAC pilot to kill six water buffaloes.

Lone gunman. In the next episode the FAC was in an F-100, and we were in North Vietnam. When we came on to the FAC's radio frequency, he advised us to use caution as the target was an enemy antiaircraft gun emplacement. We were out in the middle of nowhere and a long way from the front lines.

"What is he guarding?" I asked.

"I don't know, but I flew through here yesterday, and he shot at me."

"Why don't we let him rust out here by himself?" I suggested. We had been briefed that the enemy gave each gunner only so many rounds of ammunition each month, and when he ran out he just waited until his next ration before he could shoot again. This is one gun and one enemy in isolation.

"We have to take him out, so I'll mark his location for you."

On our second run, the gunner ran out of ammo, and we got him.

This time we won, but what happens when the gunner wins? We lose an aircraft and two pilots, or maybe the gunner gets really lucky and downs both aircraft. We took incredible risks for gains of dubious value. Does it make sense?

Cluster bombs. The last mission in this series was to a village less than fifty miles north of Danang. From the sea going inland was a miles-long beach. Sand dunes fringed with tall grass lay between the sea and the village going from east to west. The villages stretched from north to south for miles separating the dunes from the rice fields. The FAC brought us in from the sea and fired a Willy Pete into a village in the middle of all the other villages. This was in South Vietnam. We were carrying canisters of cluster bombs. The canisters blew open five-hundred feet above the ground, spreading baseball-sized, time-capsule bombs over a large circumference. These are like hand grenades, except they arm in flight and explode sporadically for the next twelve hours. When they explode they fill the air with small BB-like shot. They don't kill; they wound, blind, or amputate hands and limbs. We littered the village with them.

When we returned to base, I asked the intelligence officer why we bombed that village. It looked exactly like all the rest to me. He replied that a Vietnamese tribal chief called for that strike because he believed it had Vietcong soldiers hiding there. It also had women, children, and non-Vietcong citizens. I could envision the villagers coming out of hiding after we left and those grenades going off hour after hour, perhaps in the hand of a child, who thought they were toys. I am still haunted by those thoughts.

PLEASE, DON'T TELL ME

These are some questions from the war I do *not* want answered:

- How many people did I kill?
- How many people did I wound?

- How many Vietnamese are still being killed or maimed from buried, unexploded ordnance?
- How many Americans did I kill or wound?
- What did I accomplish?
- Why didn't I protest all this when I returned?

It isn't the answers that bother me; it's the questions! Have you ever bought something and wished later you had asked the right questions about it first? I am convinced that people can handle failure better than success. The OSI man in Seville made this statement to me during our discussions: "I think if people could see themselves as they really are, they wouldn't like themselves very much." That has always been too pessimistic for my liking, but there is some truth in it. I cannot be that hard on myself. My glass is always half full, not half empty. There is another important factor to be considered, without which we are truly pitiful creatures: hope!

> "There is nothing more frightening than arrogance or ignorance in action."
>
> --Johann Wolfgang von Goethe

At one of the SAC bases, I saw this adapted quote by Johann Wolfgang von Goethe on a large poster in the Base Operations area: "There is nothing more frightening than arrogance or ignorance in action."

SOME FINAL QUESTIONS

Would we be any better off if we had the answers to all these questions? Did we do the right thing by not searching for the answers when it might have made a difference? I visited with one of the widows not long ago.

When I wrote earlier about the intertwining of lives, the following is one instance out of many I experienced.

I knew Col. Armstrong's wife lived in Dallas. I meant to call on her when I returned from Vietnam, but I didn't. I just couldn't.

Several years ago I signed in on the Web site of the 366th Tactical Fighter Wing and logged in as a member of the 480th Tactical Fighter Squadron. They were both at Danang. That is how I found Tom Moe. We were in the 480th at the same time.

A year and a half ago, I received an e-mail message: "Did you know my father, Colonel John Armstrong?" That was all it said.

I replied, "If your father was at Danang in 1967, he was my squadron commander."

Col. Armstrong's son, Tom, and I became good e-mail friends, and we still are.

Carolyn was a dental hygienist at the time, working only two days a week and now is in retirement. She worked for a periodontist about a mile from our house. One day she was cleaning a lady's teeth and, as usual, they began to discuss parts of their lives. The lady mentioned she was married to an airline pilot, and Carolyn mentioned she was married to a retired air force pilot. One thing led to another, and Carolyn discovered the lady had been Col. Armstrong's wife. She related the experience to me that night, and I was floored. What were the chances of that happening?

A few days later her son Tom called and asked if we might meet, as he was coming to Dallas for some training. He lived in College Station, Texas. I jumped at the chance and asked him to bring his mother. I told Tom my wife would like to visit with her again. We had a wonderful two-hour visit at the cafeteria. She knew how her husband had died and had accepted it. Tom told me about everything that happened after his father was killed. He really missed his father. We can never know why his dad was taken and others survived, why some were consigned to years in a prison camp and others were not.

What made the difference for Tom Moe and me? Our lives witnessed multiple traumatic events. Even if we had the answers to the questions we do not want answered, we would survive. Had we stopped to dwell on the answers, we might have faltered, but we didn't. Was it a natural instinct to bury the unbearable? Or to hide the ugliness of the truth?

> "It is through an individual's trials and insight that character is formed, and the person is transformed."
> --Lynda Paffrath

Lynda Paffrath took a marksman's shot at this issue: "It is through an individual's trials and insight that character is formed, and the person is transformed."[1]

Aha! But what direction does that character take, or of what value is the transformation? I ran across a story in a 1959 book by Bennett Serf, *The Laugh's on Me*, which illustrates one of my points.

A swarthy young contestant on a late lamented give-away show had progressed all the way to the top rung, and with each correct answer his father in Row A applauded and vociferously shouted, "Datsa my boy!"

The $64,000 question was, "Who shot Abraham Lincoln?" After an agonizing silence, the young man confessed, "I don't remember." The audience groaned . . . all but the father, that is, who hollered, "Datsa my boy!" louder than ever."

"How can you be so happy?" demanded the man seated next to him. "Don't you realize your son has just lost $64,000?"

"Datsa my boy!" repeated the father ecstatically. "He never squeal on nobody!"[2]

In this case, not squealing on others meant surviving. The dad had his priorities in the right place for his son. No amount of money was worth risking the son's life. That attitude was a conditioned response in a world where conforming to society's codes was vital. What was humorous to us was deadly serious to the father.

Military humor was no less serious in times of severe stress. We had to laugh to keep from crying. If you saw the movie *Steel Magnolias*, when Julia Roberts's character died, you vicariously experienced the suffering and pain. The cemetery scene ended in hilarious laughter, demonstrating how recovery can begin the healing process in a short period of time. It's also how we survived.

Today these lessons are available at churches across America in ministries called "Grief Recovery." They are attended by widowed, divorced, depressed, and dysfunctional people from all types of trauma. They are usually facilitated by someone who has crossed the valley and returned to build a bridge for others to follow. The best ministries are the results of trauma. We do not like to listen to people who have not been there and do not know what it is like. That is why our survival schools were taught by real people who had real life experiences.

Another example is that I was smoking three packs of cigarettes a day in 1965 when I decided to quit. I used the twelve-step program developed for Alcoholic's Anonymous and was tutored by my stepfather, who had been dry for eight years. My goal was to make it through Vietnam without smoking. I learned I only had to stop smoking one cigarette—the first one! That way there would never be a second one. I have not smoked since.

1953—Jack Drain in K-2 Korea. "Sugarfoot" on Jack's helmet was his pet name for his fianceé, Carolyn Burgess.

1953—Jack's quarters in K-2 Korea.

1953—Jack and his assigned F-84 fighter bomber in K-2 Korea.

Jack made it back again. K-2 Korea.

1953—Kim doing laundry at "the green Nile" in K-2 Korea. Notice fortified bunker in upper right.

July 1953—Jack and Dwain Breitbach celebrating their 100th mission in K-2 Korea.

1953—Carolyn Drain with Ford Victoria in Flagstaff, Arizona.

1955—Carolyn Drain on rocket and Mary Irwin standing in "Yuma Days" parade, Yuma, Arizona.

1959—Crew accompanying Jack on African adventure near Pretoria, South Africa.

1960—Suzanne Drain, Jim Elliott, Carolyn Drain, and Nina Elliott with the pink Mercury convertible south of Chateauroux, France.

1967—F-4 fighter airplane at Danang Air Base, Vietnam.

1968—Church of Christ orphanage in downtown Danang, Vietnam.

1967—Bullet-ridden U.S. spotter plane, Danang, Vietnam.

December 19, 1967—USO show with Bob Hope outside Danang Air Base, Vietnam.

January 1968—The 480th Fighter Bomber Squadron, Danang, Vietnam. Jack is first pilot at left end of front row, kneeling.

Thanksgiving 2005—Jack and Carolyn's family at Quartz Mountain, Oklahoma. Not pictured: Son, Jeff Drain and family.

Lisa Karr, Jack and Carolyn's niece who grew up in their home.

Heather Murray, Jack and Carolyn's granddaughter.

Jeff, Vickie, Allison, and Stephen Drain, Jack and Carolyn's Son and family.

From Left to Right: Lt. Bivens, Lt. Anderson, Lt. Moe (POW), Lt. Wortham (Moe's roommate—KIA with Smitty Swords)

Tom Moe prior to a mission at Danang, Vietnam.

Lt. Thomas L. Moe, jungle survival school, PhilEpines, on his way to Vietnam.

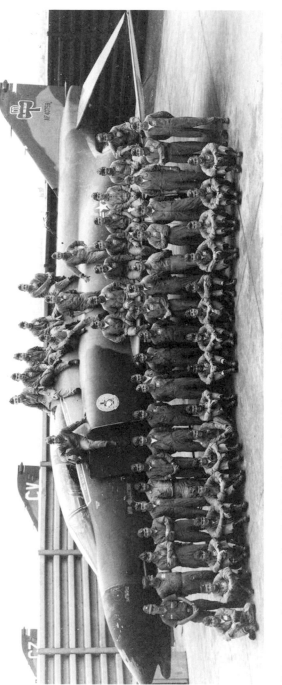

1st Row sitting, L to R: (1) Major Irvine, C Flight CO (2) Major Al Skousen, A Flight CO (3) Lt Swayze (4) Lt Lance Sijan *** (5) Lt Richard "Bob" Riddick** (6) Lt Jim Badley* (7) Major Glenn Nordin** (8) Major Donald "Scotty" Mackellar, Ops Officer (9) Majoir David C. Smith, D Flight CO (10) Lt Bobby Shannon (11) Lt Grimes (12) Lt Jim Pate**** (13) Capt Tom \Walker (14) Lt Joe Kosciusko [after war changed name to Koz] (15) Capt Johnston (16) Major Ernie Olds* 2nd Row standing, L to R: (1) Capt Tom Donal (20) Major Jack Drain, B Flight CO (3) Lt Jerry G. Koinko (4) Lt Don Wright (5) Capt Richard "Dick" Hearne (6) Capt John Martin* (7) Major Smith "Smitty" Swords* (3) Lt Tom Moe**** (9) Lt Murray Worthham* (10) Lt Col John Armstrong*, 480th TFS CO (11) Capt Norm Nielson (12) Major Rex Hammock (13) Lt John B. Flagg, Exec (14) Lt Barry Rapalus***** (15) Major Clint Moses (16) Capt Curley Savelle (17) Capt Paul Sponseller (18) Lt Les Brown (19) Capt Scot Stovin** (20) Major Bill Palmer (21) Lt Steve Demuth 3rd row sitting on the wing, L to R: (1) Lt Tom McGeehan (2) Capt Mel Pollard (3) Lt Bob Mayes (4) Lt Jack L. Kelley** (5) Major Dave Brewer (6) Lt Mark Jensen (7) Capt Lane (8) Capt Paul** 4th row sitting and standing on upper fuselage, L to R: (1) Lt Albert "Rod" Rodriguez* (sitting on intake of F-4C Phantom jet) (2) Lt McGourin (3) Lt Fielding "Wes" Featherson* (4) Lt Les Spenser (5) Lt Andy Anderson (6) Lt Gordon Jones (7) Lt Tom Howard (8) Capt Bob Gutchess (9) Major Kasischke

* Killed In Action; ** Shot down, recovered; *** Prisoner Of War, died in captivity; ****Prisoner Of War; *****Hurt when ejection seat fired on ground; **** Killed in F-4D crash in Germany in 1970. The original of this photograph is in Paul Sponseller's collection. The names of the pilots in this photo were compiled by Norml Nielsen, Glenn Nordin, John Pickitt, and Bob Riddick. Compiled by Lynda Twyman Paffrath, January 18, 2005.

Lt. Thomas Moe and squadron mates. Moe, fifth from left standing; squadron commander, Col. Armstrong (second from right standing); Lance Sijan (seated on the left); Jim Bradley (third from left, seated); Capt. Martin (third from left, standing); Murray Worthham (sixth from left, standing); Smitty Swords (fourth from left, standing), and others.

Lt. Tom Moe embraces his wife, Chris, as his 6-year-old daughter, Connie, watches. Dayton, Ohio, March 1973, on his homecoming.

Life Lessons

Let's recap some of the lessons I had learned to this point:

1. Preparing prior to exposure to traumatic events and circumstances is highly desirable.

2. Accepting what fate delivers as a natural part of life with the attitude "They can't make it too tough for me" helps us to keep from quitting.

3. Closing off what we cannot change or correct keeps us from making a career out of being victimized. It's much more than the get-over-it conundrum.

4. Realizing that we do not want all questions answered allows us to dismiss without prejudice the arenas of conflict and self condemnation. No game today! We can't lose if we don't play.

5. Recognizing the frailties and strengths of others who may have dealt with traumas about which we know nothing, allows us to identify our own frailties and strengths.

6. Sharing stories and events as observers of life builds confidence and trust among all whom we contact. Successes and failures, according to poet Edgar A. Guest, have to be treated as "imposters," since they are both threads in the fabric of life, each capable of developing character and stamina. God certainly uses our successes and failures to mold us when we place ourselves in His hands. I am trying to tell these stories with equal emphasis out of the fear that what I might consider a failure or a success was God's way of changing my course or setting the stage for the next challenging scene.

The Walking Wasted

We do our fallen comrades no service or justice when those of us who were blessed to live fail to live our lives to their fullest. Jesus said of us, "I have come that they may have life, and have it to the full" (John 10:10). In some ways our lost warriors died for Americans for a similar purpose—so we can have a full life of freedom and hope.

I went to the Fort Worth Veterans Affairs (VA) clinic to take a physical examination to determine whether I have any symptoms from exposure to Agent Orange. The planes dropping Agent Orange were loaded at Danang while I was there. We flew protective cover called "Ranch Hand missions" while C-123s dropped the deadly defoliant. Agent Orange was a chemical spray, applied much like crop-dusting chemicals, to cause the thick jungle foliage to die and fall from the trees and bushes so the enemy could not hide under the dense forestation. Approximately 20 million gallons of herbicides were used in Vietnam between 1962 and 1971. Some veterans reported a variety of health problems and concerns, which some attributed to exposure to Agent Orange or other herbicides.

My son David was born after I left Vietnam, and there was concern our children might have been affected by those chemicals. I have still not heard that they found anything amiss, so I may be one of the lucky ones. So far David shows no signs of birth defects, and he has three very healthy children. We now have eleven grandchildren, and our first grandchild, Heather, has three children, making one huge Thanksgiving celebration.

The VA waiting room was full of veterans of all wars seeking treatment. Men and women who once were required to meet dress and personal standards in appearance sometimes seem to have forgotten all of those values. They do not honor our dead by dressing like them. The "walking wasted" look like street people, and perhaps many of them are. They once were smartly dressed walking billboards for their units and their battles. Somewhere in the midst of all that has happened, they have lost their pride, self-esteem, and confidence. I also realize many may be mentally ill and not responsible for their actions. We owe all of them a great debt of gratitude, but I believe those of us who are competent owe our fallen comrades the dignity of honorable appearance.

That is a message only other veterans can send. I will not accept such criticism from a nonvet, and neither will they. Among the virtues of the America we fought for was a better life, a higher standard for ourselves and those we defended. It's true, the freedom to dress and bathe as they please are imbedded in the rights of everyone, but the personal habits in our training led us to understand the values of higher ground and responsibilities.

THE FINANCIAL WORLD

I was forty two when I retired in 1971. I did not apply for a single job that required flying skills. I did not hang out at the base or attend military social functions. We very rarely shopped at the base commissary or the base exchange. We became civilians in every sense of the word. I had never voted in a national election until after I retired. The president was my commander-in-chief, and I accepted whoever was elected by the citizens of the country. I was not active in any military associations or organizations. These were all conscious decisions. It was important for me to begin the rest of my life, and I believed the sooner I started, the better it would be.

I spent the next twenty years in the field of finance, first as a partner in a leasing company, and then as an employee of several financial institutions and banks. For two of those years I was a professional recruiter. The leasing company partnership failed in the midseventies when some of our clients went bankrupt, and we were victims of some fraudulent financial statements (no, not Enron). One of my best friends from childhood days lost a considerable amount of money in that venture. And sadly, I lost his friendship for a few years.

The 1980s basked in a gold-rush atmosphere throughout the financial world. Early in the decade there was a good deal on every corner. Financial institutions proliferated our country. New banks sprang up like *weeds*, and I use that word intentionally, because it was a disastrous development. Banks prior to that time were blessed with seasoned and competent staffs. A good banker, it was said, would not let you make a mistake in judgment that would guarantee your failure. With banks springing up so rapidly, there was no time to train and develop wise and conservative loan officers. Financial divisions in companies engaged in other industries also became lenders in the equipment-leasing fields, many without any track record or experience.

I was working for Baldwin-United during this period, developing customers for their leasing division. The goal at that time was to acquire a portfolio of equipment leases where Baldwin would own the equipment, take the investment tax credits, and the lessee would use the equipment while paying the principal and interest on the contract. Yes, this was the same company that manufactured and sold the pianos. It had become a huge conglomerate, owning banks and controlling stock interests across a rainbow of industries. They owned S&H Green Stamps and had bought a huge company called Mortgage Guaranty Insurance Company (MGIC).

My specialty was financing Burger King restaurants in the south and southwestern United States. They were in an expansion mode as well. We built about a $60 million portfolio in a few years and were set to double that in another year. Baldwin-United had wonderful employee benefits, and I took advantage of all of them. I had a nice salary, but the commissions for production far exceeded my salary. I was able to invest in their stock with a very low-interest loan and was fully invested in their profit sharing plan. One day their lenders called for payment of $950 million on their note on MGIC. Baldwin-United had planned to use the funds generated by their insurance annuity companies to pay this debt. The state insurance regulators prohibited that transaction, so Baldwin defaulted on the note. Overnight the company failed. I could not sell my stock, collect my profit sharing, and I lost my job. I still owed the company for loans on stock that now had no value. It was years before we managed to pay off that debt.

Baldwin had its headquarters in Cincinnati, Ohio. I always received a most welcome greeting from the company employees when I attended sales meetings. I lost a lot of my Texas twang while I was in the military, but I used it extensively when in Cincinnati. I always wore my cowboy boots to meetings. They loved hearing me tell jokes, and since I loved telling them, we had a mutually good deal. When the company failed we were all called up for a personnel briefing and formal notice of the final proceedings. They hosted a small banquet at a hotel across the border in Kentucky, and the briefing took place following dinner. Even though we knew what was coming, when the boss finished there was a total silence.

I stood up and said, "I guess this would not be a good time to ask for a raise?"

I stood up and said, "I guess this would not be a good time to ask for a raise?"

When the laughter subsided, I received a standing ovation, and we all celebrated our last time together. Humor has a definite place in life.

The leasing industry, along with many banks and savings-and-loan companies, declined to the point that finding financing for anyone was almost impossible. Unchecked greed and our old friends, arrogance and ignorance, reigned supreme. I had all my eggs in one basket. I struggled for two years as an independent broker, which further compounded my financial nightmare.

From 1990 to 1999 I helped build a company that processed prescription drug claims for civilian employees and military retirees. I am now fully retired and able to pursue other important endeavors. Can you see my smile?

10 From Military to Ministry

Colleyville, Texas
1980-1988

In 1980, as deacons in our church, Joe McCall and I formed (at the request of the elders) the Family Care Ministry. It is patterned after the story of the good Samaritan in the New Testament. Joe and I were the innkeepers. Apart from the church treasury, we enlisted "Samaritans," who would contribute monies for the needs of those under the oversight of our elders. Another ministry, Community Care, was assigned everyone else.

The Family Care Ministry was designed to provide grants to our members in financial distress. We raised and distributed $375,000 during the next eight years for car and house payments, medical care, food, gasoline, car repairs, and the like. The program today is even larger because of the gratitude of the people we served, who have since recovered and are now supporting the work for others. Joe and I resigned after eight years to allow others to receive the blessings we did and to bring fresh hearts to the tasks at hand. We also taught classes at church-growth seminars, helping churches all over America to form their own family care ministries.

CHAPLAIN

In 2000 my church also appointed me chaplain in order for me to have access to patients in the local hospitals. I have spent many hours visiting ill people.

I had my first heart problem in 1990, requiring angioplasty. The second came in 1993, the third in 1996, and the fourth in 1998. I had two balloon procedures and two stints installed to keep my arteries flowing blood to my heart. In 1998 I had surgery to repair a torn rotator cuff in my right shoulder. In January 2000 I had arthroscopic surgery on my left knee and a month later the same operation on the right knee. I have spent enough time in the hospital to know what it means to be a patient. I also know how a good visitor can aid in the recovery or help the patient face a medical challenge.

When I first decided to develop a visitation ministry, I spent time with a man who had been doing hospital visitation for more than ten years. He gave me his time and the benefit of his experience to help me do it right. I registered with the chaplain's office in every hospital and obtained the necessary identification tags and windshield stickers for parking.

Then I was really blessed when I met Chaplain Peggy Johnson at the North Texas Osteopathic Hospital in Fort Worth. She had a smile that could brighten the whole "valley of the shadow of death." Peggy served alone in a hospital with 220 beds and faced a workload she could not handle. She welcomed me and allowed me to make calls with her until I was comfortable doing it alone. Peggy was the wife of a local Baptist minister; they had two teenage children. When I offered to take night and weekend calls, she almost cried. We had almost a year together, Peggy on staff and I as a volunteer. She left there to provide full-time hospice services.

The visitation program turned out to be as rewarding as the Family Care Ministry. As a volunteer without limitations I could visit with each patient as long or as short a time as I thought wise. The nursing staff cooperated by briefing me on each patient, steering me to the ones who most needed encouragement or support prior to an operation and those without the support of family or friends. I could not visit patients who were under guard from the county jail, but I was allowed to call on people of all faith groups or those who had none.

I felt that every past event in my life had helped prepare me for each new challenge in some special way.

This was a chance to use my heuristic skills during traumatic events occurring all around me, but to other people for a change. I felt that every past event in my life had helped prepare me for each new challenge in some special way. Before each visit, I offered a prayer to God, asking Him to use me.

Many of the night and weekend calls were to comfort families when they had lost a loved one. Besides comfort, chaplains have a very important administrative role. Mortuaries have to be selected, decisions have to be made concerning organ and tissue donations, and occasionally the deceased has left a desire for the body to be donated to a medical school. Financial aid may be required, relatives have to be notified, and other religious support may be needed. All of that has to be appropriately timed with consolation, comfort, and sensitivity to the varied needs within a family.

CROSSING SWORDS AGAIN

On Memorial Day I received a call about daybreak to assist a lady after her husband had died. When I walked into the room, she was kneeling in prayer beside her husband's bed. I knelt down beside her and waited until she finished, and we both sat down to talk. She informed me of the situation, we had a prayer together, and I asked if she had someone she would like for me to call. They had been attending chapel services at Carswell AFB, and she wanted me to call . . . Chaplain Smitty Swords! I was barely able to contain my surprise and make the call.

Yes, it was the son of the man I wrote the efficiency report on in Vietnam. When I called the chaplain's office at the base, they confirmed that Chaplain Swords's father was indeed killed in Vietnam. He was not on base at the time, as he was conducting a memorial service in Big Spring, Texas, so I left a message for the widow and asked for the home phone number of Smitty Swords IV. Later that day I called the house and talked to Chaplain Swords's wife. She arranged our meeting when he returned from Big Spring. I told you this was bizarre.

Most of my experiences as a chaplain, as well as the dozens of stories that occurred during the Family Care Ministry, are best kept private for obvious reasons. By the way, I did not discuss this in depth, but my service as the Air Force Aid Society Officer also helped to prepare me for this ministry. I remembered times and experiences that helped me avoid a myriad of pitfalls.

I have had the wonderful blessing of performing twenty-eight weddings, six funerals, administering last rites, and comforting hundreds of scared and insecure patients when faced with life-threatening health problems. Thankfully, there were no exorcisms!

SONG OF SURVIVAL

One day, just before noon, I walked into the hospital room of a patient referred to me by the nurses. The room was dark, the shades were drawn, and the patient had her hair wrapped with a shawl and faced the wall next to the bed. I gently knocked on the wall, and the patient turned to face me. I introduced myself and offered her my services to see if she had any requests with which I could assist. She said no, but I felt that she wanted to talk some more, so I asked if I might draw a chair near to be at eye-level with her.

"That will be fine."

We talked for about ten minutes, and I learned that she lived in Fort Worth, was single, and waiting for surgery. She started asking me questions about my visitations in the hospital and how I felt about them. I answered as honestly as I could, explaining that many times there were family, friends, and religious support available, so my services were not needed.

She asked me to open the blinds, and while I did, she sat up on the edge of the bed with her feet about a foot from the floor. I was not sure if she should be doing that, but she said, "I want to do something for *you*."

I sort of stuttered and told her that she did not need to do anything for me. I was there for her.

"No," she said with a smile, "I want to sing for you."

With that announcement she released her shawl, allowing her long black hair to cascade to her waist, and began to sing a religious song, one I had never heard before.

It was absolutely beautiful! In a moment the door opened and a nurse came in, then another, and finally a third. They stood inside the door, and we all listened as she poured out her heart in a song she made up as she sang. We all applauded when she finished and she thanked us.

It turned out she was the soloist for a large downtown Baptist church. We had a good visit, and I invited her to come sing for our church. She agreed that she "just might do that." That didn't just make my day, it made my month. I still get a warm feeling when I think about her, and I know she will not mind my sharing that glorious occasion. She no longer seemed depressed when we all left.

I was in a line of one! Calling for backup was not an option.

There were situations in which I felt totally inadequate, but looking around proved my suspicions: I was in a line of one! Calling for backup was not an option. The first time I prayed beside the bed of a Catholic nun was one of those occasions. The first time I prayed beside the bed of a dying preacher who believed he was lost was another. The first time I had to inform a woman her mother had just died was heart-wrenching. These are the trenches of everyday life, and their lessons in humility and understanding surpass the exhilaration of mountaintop vistas.

DOUBLE INDEMNITY

My double knee surgery was not a success. I never did get over the pain, and it became more and more difficult to walk. In the fall of 2000, I went to see another orthopedic specialist, one with the best reputation in Fort Worth. After several visits and several tests, Dr. Schmidt turned me over to a neurologist, because he believed my pain might be coming from my back. Based on an MRI exam, Dr. Gregory Ward informed me I had a birth defect. It seems my spinal cord was tethered to my tail bone, a very rare condition and one that could only be found after 1985 when they developed the MRI. It did not show on an x-ray or the air force most likely would never have let me into pilot training. I searched the Internet for information and found a doctor who specialized in this type of corrective surgery at a Boston medical school.

Surprisingly, one of his former students was in the group of doctors with Dr. Gregory Ward. Dr. Andrea Halliday had performed several surgeries of this type and agreed to be the lead surgeon for the expected eight-hour operation to release the cord on the lower part of my spine. There was great concern that the operation could cause me to lose control of some of my functions. There was also the risk of being paralyzed for the rest of my life. As best I could discover, all of the known cases like mine were crippled by age forty, and there was only one other known patient to have this surgery past the age of sixty-five. I decided ignorance must truly be bliss, because I could not believe I had lived my life so fully and actively, not knowing I was not *supposed* to be healthy.

We had to postpone the surgery for two weeks when Dr. Halliday hurt her back. She recovered in time to make the second schedule, and on September 12, 2001, the surgery was performed. Dr. Halliday said she was able to do 100 percent of what she set out to do. I spent the next three days lying flat to let the incision heal and four more days to recover enough to be released from the hospital.

Carolyn brought me home on Thursday afternoon. The following Saturday morning Carolyn had a bad heart attack while at a beauty salon getting a permanent. She told the hairdresser "to rinse out the solution, call 911 and then Jack." I was not supposed to drive, but I beat Carolyn to the hospital, as did Suzanne and her husband, Brad, and Nicole, my granddaughter. About three hours later Carolyn was taken in for a heart catheterization, and the blockage in one artery was so bad they could not open it. She stayed in the hospital for three days, went home for a week, and returned for quadruple bypass surgery. We both had a lot of recovering to do. Family and friends made it possible for us to make it through a very scary and difficult time. I was convinced our "boat was loaded, but we were afloat on a sea of prayer."[1] Carolyn has recovered remarkably well.

While my surgery did not improve my condition, it did no harm and may have stopped me from getting worse. Needless to say it has severely limited my ability to visit people in the hospital, but it was one of the catalysts that started my writing. I also continue to perform weddings, funerals, and visitations. I was blessed and honored to perform the wedding service for my granddaughter, Nicole, who married an Army Blackhawk pilot, and he is now in Baghdad.

My good friend, Bob Ash, and I did a fundraiser for a very large congregation in our community, which crossed all denominational lines. We were then asked to help another anonymous friend distribute a significantly large contribution to the needy in our community. That led to the development of a new ministry putting benevolence back into the hands of church members. We called that one "Share the Joy." The first quarter of 2008 we funded over $100,000 in seventy-nine projects. Life is very good!

PART 2

Lighting the Fuse

To sin by silence when we
should protest makes
cowards out of men.

—ELLA WHEELER WILCOX

11 The Writing on the Wall

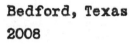

Bedford, Texas
2008

America has been and still is an open society. We have embraced the world, and it has been right and good to do so. The September 11, 2001, terrorist attacks on New York and Washington, DC, jolted us into a frightening reality previously unknown to this generation.

Many automobile accidents occur when the driver is distracted. This is no less true for a nation. We lost opportunities in the nineties due to the distractions of an immoral president and an undisciplined media. Another critical matter also needs addressing. When nations or people do not govern themselves, there is always an opportunist waiting for the chance to fill the void.

Osama bin Laden was such a person.

Afghanistan is such a nation.

Enron was such a corporation.

Democracy will collapse only from within. It will work only in a land where there is self-control and educated accountability. Judging by the myriad laws we have, it is obvious we are losing the battle of being a self-governed society. When being *legal* has more proponents than being

119

incorruptible, the writing is on the wall, just as it was for King Belshazzar when he flaunted his arrogance in the face of God (Daniel 5). The necessity to have a law for every contingency chokes the freedoms of the self-governed.

Nobel Prize-winning author Elie Wiesel once pondered how *shoah*—meaning "whirlwind" or "confusion" in Hebrew—comes about in the affairs of man. It happens, Wiesel concluded, "when good and bad are put on the same plane, and the evil receive the approval of the just."

Ongoing Questions

I am still wrestling with another troubling question from the Vienam War I'm not certain we want to have answered. The records are probably gone by now, but when I left Vietnam I calculated that we had lost twelve airplanes and twenty of their twenty-four crew members to malfunctioning bomb fuses in Danang alone.

We carried Honeywell fuses, or as Lynda Paffrath was told to call them, FMU-35 fuses. She spoke to a retired general who encouraged her not to use Honeywell's name, because "they have more clout than you do." The name means little at this point, as the only chargeable offense within the statute of limitations is murder. The fuses were defective and caused some of the bombs to explode prematurely after release, destroying both planes and crew members.

My squadron commander, Lt. Col. John Armstrong, and his GIB were among the earlier group who had their bombs blow up under the aircrafts just after release. The GIB, 1st Lt. Lance Sijan (pronounced SIGH-john), a member of my class at George AFB, was able to eject. His story of valor and resistance is included later in this book beginning on page 166. He died from complications of his POW mistreatment and the injuries received in the ejection from the plane.

Gen. Fred "Boots" Blesse, in his book *Check Six* wrote, "I do know we lost eight aircraft and crews to 'Golden BB' hits, and when we disarmed all the fuses, the losses stopped. You figure it out."[1] According to his timetable, which indicates that happened in November 1967, how do we explain the fact that Tom Moe's plane was blown out of the sky by his own bomb in January 1968?

Regardless of how many planes or how many crew members were lost, one plane and one crew member

> "I do know we lost eight aircraft and crews to 'Golden BB' hits, and when we disarmed all the fuses, the losses stopped. You figure it out."

would be enough for this story to have significant meaning. Tom survived the explosions, ejected, and called us on the emergency frequency of his two-way radio while floating down in his parachute to say that the bombs went off under their two planes. The other three crew members also ejected and were rescued. Tom was caught and imprisoned in the Hanoi Hilton for five long years. His uncommon valor and courage were acknowledged when he was introduced by vice president nominee Sarah Palin during the 2008 Republican National Convention.

What did not happen is what we are all about. It's those heuristic questions again. Every pilot at Danang knew about the fuses. The armament people knew. Our superior officers knew. It was known by generals at 7th Air Force Headquarters in Saigon. It was even reported in the official U.S. Air Force "History of 366th Tactical Wing" at Danang AB, covering 1 October–31 December 1967—a document originally classified but later declassified.

The Hanoi Hilton, Room 7

This is the history of the people who were in Room 7 at the "Hanoi Hilton."

In late 2000 CAG Stockdale, (Room 7 SRO) asked his old friend By Fuller to provide a list of the roommates of Room 7, Hanoi Hilton as of Christmas 1970. The roommates were extraordinary, both at the time of incarceration, and then later in freedom.

Room 7 had the first organized church service to be held in the prisons of North Vietnam. Permission was asked for by Stockdale and twice denied by the Camp Commander. The room was warned not to do it. Room 7 decided to do it anyway. They even had a choir.

Their solemn service quickly caught the eye of the guards and authorities. Armed guards rushed into the room to break up the "ominous" unauthorized meeting. Ringleaders Risner, Coker, and Rutledge were led out of the room with guards at each arm (they were headed for more Heartbreak Hotel, solitary confinement and lots of punishment).

Bud Day was the one who then jumped up on his bed and started to sing the national anthem and "God Bless America." The entire room burst into song. Then Rooms 6, 5, 4, 3, 2, and 1 joined into the songs in succession. These songs of pride and defiance were loud enough to be heard outside the fifteen-foot walls of the Hanoi Hilton. As Robbie marched out the door, his back straightened with pride. He held his head high.

Robbie later recalled his thoughts as his roommates burst out in song: "I felt like I was nine feet tall and could go bear hunting with a switch."

Thirty-one years later, on November 16, 2001, a nine-foot-tall bronze statue of Brigadier General Robinson Risner, USAF, would be dedicated on the central plaza of the United States Air Force Academy. To Bud Day (principal speaker), Ross Perot (sponsor of the project), and dozens of Robbie's Room 7 roommates at the ceremony, it seemed more fitting to call the statue "life-size."

CAG, knowing what the V [Vietcong] reaction would be, was heard to remark something to the effect, "Well, I guess we just can't stand prosperity." Our camp, yet unnamed, from that moment on became known as "Camp Unity."

The guards protested, but the songs continued. Shortly thereafter, Vietnamese troops entered each room in force. They had their hats secured with chinstraps in place, they had fixed bayonets, and they were mad! They quickly backed the POWs against the walls with a bayonet in each POW's stomach. The singing immediately ceased as the troops burst through the doors. The V later claimed they had put down a riot. It wasn't a real riot, but it was a lot of fun . . . until the soldiers entered the room.

Several roommates of Room 7 were jerked out the next day. Then Orson Swindle in Room 6 tapped the following message on the wall: "Damn, you'd have to get in line to get in trouble in that crowd!"

Thanks to By Fuller for the work of putting together these facts. Paul Galanti and Mike McGrath assisted. This historical document is dedicated to a fearless leader, Vice Admiral Jim Stockdale, CAG.

Here are some of what the men of Room 7 accomplished:

Total days in captivity: 108,116
Man-years in captivity: 296.21

Here's a brief history of the 47 men:

- 5 Made Admiral rank (Stockdale O-9, Lawrence O-9, Shumaker O-8, Denton O-8, Fuller O-8).
- 1 Made General rank (Risner O-7)
- 40 Others stayed in the military and attained the following ranks:
- USMC 1 Colonel (Dunn)
- Navy 1 Commander (Coker)
- Air Force 1 Lt. Colonel (Daughtrey)
- Air Force 19 Colonels (Craner, Crow, Crumpler, Day, Dramesi, Finlay, Guarino, Gutterson, Hughes, Kasler, Johnson, Kirk, Lamar, Larson, Ligon, McKnight, Pollard, Stockman, & Webb)
- Navy 18 Captains (Brady, Coskey, Crayton, Daniels, Doremus, Fellowes, Franke, Gillespie, James, Jenkins, McCain, Moore, Mulligan, Rivers, Rutledge, Schoeffel, Stratton, and Tanner)
- 2 Became U.S. Congressmen (Johnson, Texas; McCain, Arizona).
- 2 Became U.S. Senators (Denton, Alabama; McCain, Arizona).
- 1 Was a vice presidential candidate (Stockdale).
- 1 Was a presidential candidate (McCain) 2008.
- 2 Received the Medal of Honor (Stockdale, Day). Day resumed his career as a lawyer.
- 3 Received the Navy Cross (Denton, Coker, Fuller). (3 of the 4 POWs to receive this award were from this room. Red McDaniel was the 4th POW to receive the award).
- 4 Made escapes. All were recaptured; all were tortured. (Dramesi, Coker, McKnight, Day)

- 2 were jet aces from the Korean War (Risner—9 kills in F-86; Kasler—6 kills in F-86)
- 1 First pilot to fly over Russia in U-2 spy aircraft (Stockman).
- 1 Was shot down 4-15-1944 in Germany. POW until April 1945. 26th mission in P-47 (Ligon).
- 1 Shot down 3 German planes during WW II. Flying British aircraft. (Guarino) Flew 156 missions in Sicily, India, China and Indo-China.
- 1 Flew 62 missions in Korean War. Got credit for 1 kill, 1 damaged, 1 probable kill against Mig-15s (Johnson).
- 8 Received Distinguished Service Medals (Shumaker, Denton, Crayton, Stockdale, Lawrence, Day, Guarino, and Riser).
- 7 Received the U. S. Air Force Cross (Kasler—3 awards; Risner—2 awards; Dramesi—2 awards, Day, Kirk, Guarino, and McKnight each received one award).
- 4 Were Navy Test Pilots (Stockdale, Lawrence, Gillespie, and Franke).
- 1 Flew with the Thunderbirds (Johnson)
- 11 Were USNA graduates (Brady '51, Denton '47, Fellowes '56, Fuller '51, Gillespie '51, Lawrence '51, McCain '58, Rivers '52, Schoeffel '54, Shumaker '56, & Stockdale '47).
- 2 Were Landing Signal Officers (LSOs) (Stockdale, Tanner).
- 1 Escaped the B-52 community and got into combat flying the F-105G (Larson).
- 1 Has a daughter who is an astronaut, gone into space three times (789 hours). She flew as a crewmember of the International Space Station (Lawrence).
- 1 Was a Navy Air Wing Commander (CAG): (Stockdale—COMAIR-GRU 16).
- 1 Commanded a Navy Carrier, USS *America*. Later became Battle Group Commander—CARGRU 4 Commander (Fuller).
- 10 Were Squadron Commanders (Coskey (VA-85), Day (TBD), Denton (VA-75), Franke, Fuller (VA-76), Gillespie, Jenkins VA-163), Lawrence (VF-143), Ligon (11th TRS) and Larson (469th TFS) when shot down), Schoeffel (VA-83).
- 5 Were Squadron Executive Officers (Daniels, Moore, Mulligan, Rutledge, and Brady).
- 10 Authored books:
    a. Day: *Return with Honor*
    b. Denton: *When Hell Was In Session*
    c. Dramesi: *Code of Honor*
    d. Guarino: *A POW's Story: 2801 Days in Hanoi*

e. Johnson: *Captive Warriors: A Vietnam POW's Story*
f. McCain: *Faith of My Fathers*
g. Mulligan: *The Hanoi Commitment*
h. Risner: *The Passing of the Night*
i. Rutledge: *In the Presence of Mine Enemies*
j. Stockdale: *Courage Under Fire; In Love and War; A Vietnam Experience; Thoughts of a Philosophical Fighter Pilot.*

- 4 Became presidents/commandants/superintendents of institutions of higher learning: (Stockdale: President of the Citadel and President of the Naval War College; Lawrence: Superintendent of the USNA; Shumaker: Superintendent of the Naval Postgraduate School; and . . . (TBD) . . .; Denton: Commandant of Armed Forces Staff College).
- 2 Built their own airplanes (Jenkins—LongEZ; Shumaker—Lancaire). Pollard is currently flying sail planes. CAPT (Commodore) Harry Jenkins commanded PHIBRON Five, aboard *USS Tripoli* (LPH-10), 1977–78).
- 1 Was the first active duty Naval Aviator to fly Mach II (Lawrence).
- 1 Was first Naval Aviator to land on an aircraft carrier in 0/0 fog with a newly developed Aircraft Carrier Landing System (Gillespie). Yes, it was an emergency low fuel state!
- 2 Naval Aviators were in the final selection groups (before shootdown) for the Mercury Astronaut Program (Lawrence, Shumaker).
- Many of the members of Room 7 either served during wars prior to Vietnam or saw combat in theatres other than Vietnam:

WWII:
Vern Ligon: USA Air Corps, 25 missions, P-47 pilot, POW in Stalag Luft 1, 1944–45, escaped once, recaptured.
Larry Guarino: USA Air Corps, 156 missions in Sicily, India, China and Indo-China. Spitfires.
Hervey Stockman: USA Air Corps. 68 missions, P-51.
Jim Kasler: USA Air Corps, 7 missions as tail gunner, B-29.
Harry Jenkins & Gordon Larson were Navy V5 cadets . . . and Fred Crow was an Army Air Corps aviation cadet when WWII ended.
Bud Day: Corporal, USMC, 30 months in south and central Pacific, April 1942–Nov. 1945.
By Fuller and Carl Crumpler: Enlisted in US Navy summer of 1945. Saw boot camp the the end of WW II.
Fred Crow and Al Brady: were Navy dependents at Pearl Harbor, December 7, 1941.

Korea:
Robby Risner: USAF, 108 missions, F-86. Mig Ace with 9 kills.
Jim Kasler: USA, 100 missions, F-86, Mig Ace with 6 kills.
Howie Rutledge: USN, 200 missions, F9F-2 as a Flying Midshipman.
Harry Jenkins: Served aboard *USS Fred T. Berry* (DD-141) off coast of
Korea. These Naval Aviators were known as "Flying Midshipman."
Tom Kirk: Flew missions in Korea, Air Force Cross
Larry Guarino: USAF, Air Defense Alert missions.
Jim Lamar: USAF, 100 missions in F-80 and P-51.
Wendy Rivers: Served on a destroyer off the coast of Korea.
Laird Gutterson: USAF, flew 60 missions, P-51.
Verlyne Daniels: Flew AD-4 missions, March–August 1953.
Sam Johnson: USAF, flew 62 missions, F-86, 1 kill, 1 probable, 1 damaged
against Mig 15s.
Bud Day: USAF, air defense missions, F-84s.
Bill Lawrence (F2H-3) and By Fuller (F9F-5) arrived off the coast of Korea
in October 1953. They were flying off the *USS Oriskany*. Too late . . . the
war was over!
Fred Crow: Had flight orders to Korea cancelled as war ended. Served
stateside flying F-86.
Carl Crumpler: Flew F-86s at George AFB. War was over too soon for him
to participate.

Magnificent men, whether in a cockpit, in a cell, or at a desk! This information is provided to show that, regardless of the circumstances, some
men are never defeated, only temporarily delayed.[2]

In part the declassified air force document reported this:

> We lost three and possibly four to enemy anti-aircraft reaction. The
> exact cause for loss of the remaining three aircraft is not known.
> These aircraft were all carrying FMU35 fuzed [sic] weapons, so the
> possibility of a malfunction was considered. We discontinued tem-
> porarily the use of the FMU35 fuze [sic] and technical assistance was
> requested to pursue the problem.

Who did *not* know? Sadly, some of the wives of the lost crew members *still* do not know!

The Writing on the Wall

Not one of us called the press, called the widows, or wrote the stories. Did it die? Or did it reach McNamara? If so, did it reach President Johnson? You may remember that President Johnson did not run for re-election. Historians say that the war in Vietnam caused him to leave office without a fight. Was this tragedy over the fuses one of the contributing reasons? Did he believe this would come out in an election year and destroy his credibility? I've shot all around it, but I do not know which bullet may have hit either one of them. McNamara has recanted most of his role in the Vietnam War, but I did not see this issue discussed.

Whose Fault Was It?

Another critical question comes to mind: who caused the fuses to be defective? Was it the engineer, who designed and developed them? Was it some assembly line employee, who did not understand how they were to be assembled? Was it an inspector, who did not catch the error before signing off on them? Was it an air force contracting officer, who had an incompetent quality control officer? Perhaps it was just part of Murphy's Law.

Lynda Paffrath tells the defective fuse story from the perspective of her friend, Jim Badley, as follows:

Jim's new Aircraft Commander was Major Dennis Harper, who had arrived at Danang in the early part of November and had just recently completed the extensive training and indoctrination courses. They flew one mission together before Jim was sent to Hong Kong on November 23, 1967, for a much needed R & R.

Jim returned to Danang on November 26, 1967, and was immediately given some bad news. 1st/Lt. Doug Condit, a good friend of Jim's from college, and Colonel Bert Brennan had just been shot down in Laos. It seemed to be a repeat performance of Colonel John

Armstrong's and 1st/Lt. Lance Sijan's shoot down two weeks earlier. They had rolled in on the target, released their bombs, and had immediately blown up. Bert and Doug were shot down in an area that wasn't known to be that hot in terms of antiaircraft fire, so it was suspected that the FMU-35 fuses had been defective once again.

Colonel Frederick "Boots" Blesse, Deputy Commander of Operations for the wing, had immediately suspected the fuses after the back-to-back tragedies of Colonel Armstrong's flight and Baffle Flight. (Baffle Flight had disappeared from the ground controller's radar screen at the exact moment of bomb release. Air force authorities "explained away" the disappearance as having been the result of a "midair collision." None of us pilots accepted that theory. At that time Colonel Blesse had ordered all the FMU-35 fuses removed and replaced with regular bombs. Unfortunately, Seventh Air Force Headquarters in Saigon didn't agree with Col. Blesse's conclusion that the FMU-35 fuses were at fault. Headquarters said that it was an unfortunate coincidence that both flights blew up on release of their bombs, but the circumstantial evidence didn't warrant suspending use of the FMU-35 fused bombs. Furthermore, Seventh Air Force reminded Colonel Blesse that there was a dire need for this ordnance in the war, and they ordered him to resume use of the FMU-35 fused bombs. Colonel Blesse couldn't refuse a direct order, so the wing resumed use of the FMU-35 fused weapons. Bert Brennan and Doug Condit were one of the first crews to use the bombs after the wing put them back in service.

The Writing on the Wall

After Colonel Brennan and Lt. Condit's flight was blown up, Colonel Blesse ordered use of the FMU-35 fuses suspended until a thorough investigation could be conducted. This time Seventh Air Force listened and responded to him by sending U.S. Air Force Contractor personnel to Danang to officially investigate the fuse problem This official investigation couldn't find anything wrong with the fuses, and delivery of the weapons employing this fuse was commenced the end of December.

Two weeks later on January 16, 1968, Col. Blesse's suspicions were finally confirmed. On that day Capt. Charles Lewis and Lt. Jack Kelly were assigned to a sky spotting mission using the FMU-35 fuses; the nine bombs were set for delayed detonations from forty-five minutes to six hours. Kelley was very concerned about the fuses, so during the briefing he advised Capt. Lewis to take the extra precaution of pulling up sharply upon release of the last bomb and, fortunately, that was precisely what he did.

Later, Capt. Lewis described what ensued three-quarters of a second after the last bomb was dropped: "Then BAM it happened. There was no doubt in our minds as to what happened—one of our bombs below and behind our right wing had exploded. We saw the flash of light, felt the push on the aircraft, heard the noise, and saw about one-third of our right wing being blown in pieces up and slightly to the left."

Capt. Lewis and Lt. Kelley safely ejected and were rescued several hours later. After they returned to base, the two rescued crewmen told how the FMU-35 fuses had prematurely detonated the bombs, which destroyed their aircraft. And that was all the proof Colonel Blesse personally needed—he ordered the armament people to use the fuses, but to leave them disconnected from the bombs. From that time forward there were no more incidents at Danang of aircraft suddenly blowing up upon release of its bombs, which were armed by FMU-35 fuses.[3]

Now, let's compare Lynda's account with Gen. Blesse's version in his book *Check Six*.

Between 9 and 20 November, we lost several other aircraft. As in the case of Armstrong and Sijan, they were "Golden BB" losses—roll into a dive, explosion, no survivors. We tried to stop flying and investigate our procedures, but we had no proof that anything was wrong. As we were told, sometimes you get losses like those in combat.

Bert had the last R & R, so I decided to take a few days off and go to Hong Kong. He kidded me about passing me in total missions, but that didn't matter; I just felt I needed a change. On 22 November I was in Hong Kong and it was magnificent. I slept late, bargained with the merchants, and ate in fine restaurants for four luxurious days. On the 25th I climbed aboard the transport and headed back to Danang with a doorknob in each hand, leaving heel marks all the way.

Fred Haeffner met me, as Bert was busy in Ops. The first news I got was that we lost a couple more aircraft and crews–same conditions. I wanted to fly. Fred assured me that was no problem and said he would notify my back seater, Doug Condit. It would be the mid-morning mission. Fred deposited me at my trailer, and I decided to unpack everything before going to lunch. A few minutes later Bert came in, and we carried on like I had been gone a month or so. Bert was as fine a guy as I ever met. With a good sense of humor, bright and capable, he had that rare ability to inspire others to do better than they knew how.

"Well, Bert," I said after a couple of subjects were discussed quickly, "how many missions did you get while I was in Hong Kong?"

"Not one damn flight," Bert said, "The boss has had a burr under his saddle ever since you left."

I thought about that for a moment and then recounted to Bert about being on the flight schedule for the next day.

"Bert, it doesn't seem fair to me to be in Hong Kong four days and then come back and fly before you do. Why don't you take the mission instead? Doug is all set up to go. I know he would enjoy going with you."

"Hey, boss, that's great," Bert said. "I really appreciate it." And that settled it."

Col. Blesse goes on to tell about the loss of Bert and Doug and his remorse in the next paragraph and then he relates this:

About a week later we were scheduled for a mission we called "Skyspot." The aircraft flew to a designated point at which they were picked up by radar. They were then vectored, heading and distance, to another point from which a countdown began. Seconds later the radar controller called for bomb release, and all four aircraft would comply. This procedure was generally used during overcast conditions to keep the enemy ducking even in bad weather.

One of our four ship flights received a hurry-up vector, and as a result were still spread out when the countdown began. Generally, the aircraft would be within a few feet of each

At least twelve aircraft, if not more, and twenty lost crewmen prove not *all* the fuses were good.

other, but this time the third and fourth men were several hundred yards away when the command was received to release bombs. As the leader released, three and four observed the go and saw one explode a few feet under the aircraft. They got the message back, and we immediately grounded everything until we could determine the problem. We lost the leader and his wingman—four aircrew.

We reasoned the cause had to do with fusing, but we couldn't get anyone in higher headquarters to agree. We had to continue to carry them, but no one said they had to be armed—so we had the fuses disarmed and tried that for a while. The losses stopped.[4]

In comparing these two versions of the story for consistency, you'll notice that Lynda failed to include a third and fourth aircraft and did not mention that Tom Moe and Scott Stovin were in the other aircraft or that Tom was captured. Col. Blesse does not mention that three of the four crewmen were rescued or that Tom was captured. One thing is apparent: not all the fuses were bad. I flew several missions with them and do not know that any of them detonated prematurely. Just as obvious is that some *were* defective. I assume the team sent by 7th Air Force to investigate was from Honeywell. I cannot imagine anyone else being qualified to investigate. Perhaps the fuses they checked were good. At least twelve aircraft, if not more, and twenty lost crewmen prove not all the fuses were good.

Tom Moe added this version of the story:

Linda cites the incident of Lewis and Kelly in F-4C tail number 64-0927. That was the flight that I too was a part of. Col. Blesse was wrong on a number of counts. The flight was a two-ship flight; it had never been scheduled as a four-ship. In fact we flew few if any four-ship missions. Secondly, the flight was spread because we did not trust the fuses (not because there was some last-minute regrouping due to miscommunication).

As Linda states, the FMU-35 was "cleared for use," and our flight was the first one to use it following the decision. We were a flight of two—call sign "Hangar Flight." We were well aware of the fuse problem, so we jokingly called ourselves "Guinea Pig Flight." Lewis and Kelly were flying number two. By the way, I recall quite clearly that Lewis was a major, not a captain.

Flying number one was Captain Scott Stovin (front seater) and I (GIB) in F4-D tail number 66-8706. Stovin had been an ATC instructor before being retrained in the F-4. He had no previous experience in fighters, and like many of these "retreads" had less time than we GIBS who had entered fighters right out of pilot training. We too were relatively inexperienced compared to other career fighter pilots, but had nearly all our flying time in combat. Thus the practice was to put more experienced GIBs, like Kelly and me, with the retreads until they got up to speed.

Knowing the danger we faced with the faulty fuses, we briefed that we would drop our ordnance from high altitude, in a wide-spread formation and pull up at bomb release in order to increase separation as much as possible and as quickly as possible between ourselves and the bombs. Had we not done so, we surely would have been blown to bits just as Baffle Flight was.

My fate to become a POW was sealed when we were diverted from our planned target, which was on the coast, to a self-chosen target far inland. We had hoped to set up a west-to-east pass so that we were headed for the Gulf on Tonkin at bomb release. The method of delivery was to be using a system called "Magic" or "MISCUE"—an acronym for something that I have long-since forgotten.

The missions were categorized as a "sky spot" mission as Blesse points out. A ground controller would receive a signal from our "Magic" system and guide us to bomb delivery. However, as we approached the target, we were diverted, because had to fly too close to an artillery fan being issued by the USS *Canberra* offshore to permit us to guide ourselves. We were directed to choose another target away from the artillery fan. As we set up for that delivery, the ground controller could not receive the signal from our "Magic" system and ordered us to deliver our ordnance using our own TACAN. The nearest target was inland and located about ninety miles east of the Nakom Phenom TACAN.

As we counted down for bomb release, Scott forgot to begin his pull up. I grabbed the stick and yanked hard, pulling up even to the already pulling wingman just as his bomb predetonated. The rear of his aircraft was immediately engulfed in flames, and he began to dutch roll as his airframe disintegrated. I had to maneuver our aircraft to avoid a midair, even though we had been separated by several hundred feet at bomb release. Soon number 2's tail broke off, and the aircraft began a violent spin—so violent that the spinning nose created a vapor trail. I watched as Kelly ejected before the aircraft disappeared into the undercast.

Moments later I smelled smoke, and Scott hollered that his fire lights had lit up. He called for an ejection, but the aircraft rolled inverted. I told him I did not want to eject inverted so I hauled aft on the stick and pushed full rudder to roll the aircraft erect. Our flight control hydraulics had failed, PC 1 and 2, so I had no aileron authority. Holding the aircraft erect with full aft stick and full rudder, Scott took control so that I could eject. Ejection went okay, although being at high altitude I had to ride my seat down to about 18,000 feet to the point where the chute automatically deployed.

Once I was finally dangling in my chute, I got on my survival radio and relayed what had happened to another flight. At first the pilots in that flight did not know that I was speaking to them in my parachute. I related what happened to them, and they radioed head-quarters with the information. HQ immediately grounded the fuse and recalled other aircraft that had already taken off with the fuse, thus averting further tragedy.

Having thus provided the first surviving eyewitness account of the fuse malfunction, I turned my attention to my own survival as I entered the undercast. A hostile welcome greeted me as I popped out from the clouds and immediately attracted small arms fire from unseen enemy troops in the dense jungle I was to learn over the next three days, as I evaded the enemy on the ground, that I had come down near an antiaircraft site, which was manned by dozens of troops.[5]

I asked a retired lawyer, Jim Jameson, to read the draft of this book. Here are some of his comments:

This is a very interesting story, and I am glad that you have written it . . . . I probably would have been put before the firing squad if I had been confronted with the Honeywell fuse problem . . . When Vietnam was closing, the "boys" were coming back and trying to reconstruct their lives. Not one officer came to me for legal help in job-related incidents. All I saw were the boys who went into those jungles at night, fought in the dark, were subjected to orders that never made sense and treated as if they were expendable. They were scared in

Vietnam; they were scared when they came home to reconstruct; and many were still scared, shaky, nervous, and unable to hold jobs. Much depression and many job-related problems. It just made me furious when I thought about why we were in Vietnam, why we stayed in Vietnam, and the total lack of concern for the welfare of the soldiers by the Veterans Administration.[6]

Here is my response, in part, to Jim:

Tom Moe went to three attorneys with his story about the fuses. They all turned him down, refusing to take his case, in view of the difficulty tracing the story and getting evidence to prove it. Furthermore, there was a strong likelihood that specific fault could not be found. There may have been governmental protection for the manufacturers of ordnances due to the high risk in handling and distribution.

Your expressed anger over the fuse incident is one of the goals of our writing. Exposing the arrogance of those in command and their refusal to accept/acknowledge responsibility or to conduct a thorough investigation is another of our goals.

All of us who knew about this went on to successfully complete our careers, even Tom. There is a strong possibility that those futures would have not been possible had we fought that battle. Where should the battle have been fought? By whom? Those are additional unanswered questions.

Jim wrote back:

A quick response on the fuses. By this time, there must be data on the defective fuses . . . Honeywell will contend that if the fuses were defective, then it is the problem of the Defense Department, as Honeywell manufactured them according to specifications. The Freedom of Information Act might provide a lead. A search of products liability cases that *might* be in the archives of the American Trial Lawyers Association might yield something. A letter to the magazine published by the American Trial Lawyers might arouse someone who has information . . . I will place a call to ATLA to see if they can give me any leads.

There is no right place to go for this information. One might happen to find a lawyer dedicated to the investigation, or sometimes a posting on the Internet will uncover something of value. Surely there is someone out there with a conscience.[7]

Agreeing with Jim, I decided to do some investigating on my own.

12 A Relentless Search

6:00 a.m.
Monday
18 February 2002

The need for documentation and "proof" that the fuses were, indeed, defective and that the powers that be knew it and covered it up ate away at me like acid. I felt I owed it to the men whose losses were shoved into an obscure file drawer and intentionally forgotten. So Jim's encouragement led me to try again to find something on the Internet. Success! My search finally turned up a significant link to Phil Ratté, then a candidate for the Independence Party for state representative in District 52A in Minnesota.

Among other jobs Ratté had worked for Honeywell during his last two years of engineering school and for two years while in graduate school. He was a production engineer in the Ordnance Division, making various fuses for explosive devices. Phil's ideas saved taxpayers more than a million dollars a year. The contract Ratté worked on became the most profitable contract in the Ordnance Division. The contract produced bomb fuses for the 500-pound bombs used in Vietnam. He and his team simplified the design of the fuse so that it was not a "dud" on hard impact, and it cost 60 percent less.

I have to wonder at the *coincidence* of his running for office and my looking for him at the same time. Is it possible my opening remark about "the dead crying out to us" was more truth than I could have ever imagined? Has anyone ever researched a thirty-four-year-old subject and had it come alive at the very moment he was looking for answers? If my writing had influenced a reader somewhere, I could understand a response, but at this stage of the writing there were only four people who had seen any of this manuscript: Carolyn; Pat Nimmo Riddle, who was doing the first edit; Jim Jameson; and me. Tom Moe had seen the first draft of two and a half pages, but they had since been rewritten. Lynda Paffrath had not seen any of it.

8:45 p.m.
Monday
18 February 2002

Lynda Paffrath sent me the following e-mail:

> How in the world did you find this guy? He's certainly the right age and right time in terms of working at Honeywell when the fuses were being developed. And he certainly doesn't sound like the type of individual who would let anything slip by him, so there's a chance he heard all about the fuse problem, even if he wasn't the one working directly on them.
>
> You're right about proceeding with caution. Someone with infinite tact and mental agility will have to approach this guy.
>
> Congratulations, Jack. Good research material. Maybe he'd be willing to help.[1]

I went back to the source where I had found the information on Ratté to see if there were other gems of information, and I found this enlightening article:

A Relentless Search

Laos Facing Decades of Unexploded Bombs

by Daniel Lovering, *Boston Globe* Correspondent

June 11, 2000, PAKSONG, Laos: Standing on this jungle plateau in southern Laos, Pong Inthisane takes stock of the day's work: two 500-pound bombs, 20 antitank rockets, and scores of rusting mortars, all neatly stacked at his feet. Glancing at his notepad as if referring to a familiar recipe, he inspects a wad of plastic explosive stuck to the bombs, and nods approvingly. It's time to blow them up.

"I don't remember how many times I've done this," said Inthisane, 27, a team leader with Laos's bomb disposal program, UXO Lao, as he heads down a dusty path to a protective log bunker.

For Inthisane, destroying the leftovers of war is a daily routine in this corner of Laos bordering Cambodia and Thailand.

Twenty-five years after the Vietnam War, Laos is still battling one of the war's worst legacies: unexploded bombs. From 1964 to 1973 the United States dropped about 2 million tons of bombs along the Ho Chi Minh Trail, the North Veitnamese supply route that snaked through the jungles of eastern Laos. An average of one planeload of bombs fell every eight minutes for nine years, according to government records. Bomb specialists and manufacturers estimate that *up to 30 percent of them did not explode because they were dropped at an altitude too low or simply malfunctioned.*

Since the war, unexploded bombs in bamboo thickets and rice fields have posed a constant threat. Accidental explosions have killed or maimed more than 10,000 people since the war, and broad swaths of valuable farmland are too dangerous to cultivate. About 25 percent of all villages in Laos are contaminated, according to a 1997 study by Handicap International, a humanitarian agency based in Brussels.

Many bombs are small antipersonnel devices from U.S.-made cluster bombs. Millions of the tennis-ball-size "bombies," as they are known locally, litter the countryside, along with an array of munitions from Vietnam, France, and other nations that waged war in Indochina during the past half-century.

Thonglay Thammavong, 46, discovered a bombie in 1986 while digging a latrine behind his family's thatched hut in Sekong, near the former Ho Chi Minh Trail.

He struck the ground with his hoe and dug until he saw what he thought was fruit.

"I knocked it with a piece of bamboo," Thammauong said, "then I decided to throw it away."

When Thammavong cocked his arm to hurl the bomblet, it exploded. He was knocked unconscious for a few minutes until his family found him and carried him to a hospital.

"They cut my hand off," he said pointing to a nub just below his elbow, covered with a patch of black cotton.

Accidents like Thammavong's are less common, thanks to awareness programs and the systematic removal of unexploded ordnance, or UXO, from populated areas.

UXO Lao started five years ago with the support of the United Nations Development Program. With $12 million in equipment and monetary contributions from 11 countries, UXO Lao is run by the communist Lao government and advised by six international bomb clearance groups. Twenty-nine bomb-disposal specialists from Britain, Norway, and elsewhere work with 1,015 Lao staff. By the end of 2002, when the UN contract ends, the Lao government wants to withdraw most of UXO Lao's foreign advisers to become more self-sufficient. But some advisors say that while the Lao mine-sweepers have performed admirably, they are not ready to take over because they lack decision-making skills—a consequence of living under an authoritarian regime that discourages critical thinking—and technical knowledge to cope with the abundance of ordnance in Laos.

Many of the bombs were manufactured in the United States by Honeywell and Hayes International. Some have sophisticated fuses still classified by the U.S. government. Until two years ago the US government ignored the bombs it left behind in Laos. "The cleanup of ordnance is the responsibility of the people who caused the conflict," said one Pentagon official recently.

"Just because we dropped the stuff doesn't mean we're going to go in there and clean it up."

Exactly who started the conflict in Laos, may be a matter of debate. But there is no question about its escalation. The CIA secretly orchestrated a civil war against communist forces in Laos long before the Vietnam War broke out. Airstrikes followed as fighting ensued in neighboring Vietnam. Regardless of its cleanup policy, the United States has become UXO Laos's biggest supplier of training and equipment, such as trucks, mine detectors, and computers.

From 1997 through 1999, the US sent troops to Laos to teach de-mining at a UXO Lao training camp, a program some say was ill-advised because it emphasized land mines rather than bombs. Land mines represent about 4 percent of the explosives in Laos.

"They were teaching them the American mine clearance drill, which we do not use," said Erik Tollefsen, a field manager with Norwegian People's Aid, an agency that has advised UXO Lao since 1997. "They're good teachers using typical military instruction, but their doctrine is wrong."

In 1998 the US government contributed $750,000 to UXO Lao for a US contractor to teach advanced bomb disposal.

"They'll have work for 50 or 100 years," said Joe DeVroe, a Belgian bomb specialist and UXO Lao adviser. "We still find ammunition in Belgium from the first World War—more than 80 years after the war—so why should it be any different in Laos?"[2] (italics mine)

God, it seems, was directing our course.

God, it seems, was directing our course. Lynda and I were concerned about how to proceed when a door opened, providing us a natural cover for contacting Mr. Ratté. I decided to prepare for a telephone interview and hoped Mr. Ratté would allow me to record it. We hoped it would not backfire on us.

PLANNING THE INTERVIEW

Here is the interview I prepared to use with Phil Ratté:

"Hello. Mr. Ratté, please."

"Mr. Ratté, this is Jack Drain. I'm writing some material on the aftermath of the Vietnam War. I ran across some statistics that might interest my readers on your campaign Web site, and I wondered if you might be of some help. The statistic in question is, according to an article in the *Houston Chronicle*, of the 2 million tons of bombs dropped in Vietnam and neighboring countries, some 30 percent of them did not explode. Of course, the focus is on what is happening today—that those bombs are having to be destroyed, and people are still being killed.

"When I saw your site, I read that you worked on the fuses to try and cure that situation. Do you have time to discuss this with me, or should I call back later?

"Great! I would like to record your information, if you don't mind. That way I won't have to keep calling to verify my understanding of what you said.

"Thanks, I appreciate that. In order to cut my phone bill down and not waste your time, I have prepared a series of questions that will get us through as soon as possible. By the way, you certainly have an interesting resumé of qualifications.

1. When is the election day? It didn't say on the Web site.
2. Do you have a tough opponent?
3. Isn't your governor a member of the Independence Party?
4. How long did you work for Honeywell? Long enough to retire?
5. I think my readers will have an interest in the background of those statistics. How do they know 30 percent of the bombs did not explode? Would you discuss that for us?
6. I know we have experts on defusing bombs, but I understand some cannot be defused. Would you comment on that?
7. What did you or Honeywell think was the problem of the bombs not exploding?
8. Were you in on this from the beginning? I mean the research and analysis? Were there others?
9. Do you think any of them are still alive? Have you kept in touch with them? Do you think they would mind if I called them as well?
10. Is any of this still classified as "secret"?
11. How did your fuse solve the problem?
12. How was it tested and where?
13. This fuse you developed—was it a new design or a modification to an existing fuse?
14. Did your fuse have a military nomenclature, number, or designation?
15. What percentage of your fuses did not explode the bombs?
16. How do you keep a bomb from detonating before you want it to?

17. Why were the old fuses failing? Were they Honeywell fuses as well?

18. Did you get a nice bonus or promotion from your design? Do you own the patents or did Honeywell keep them?

19. Why was it such a profitable item if it saved the taxpayers money? Did your fuse replace one that another company was making for the government?

20. I certainly appreciate your time and information. Is there anyone else you might suggest I call for more details on the usage of the fuses? Did you have a military contact? Do you recall any names or titles?

21. Well, sir, thank you for your help. May I call you again if I get stuck?

22. Do I have your permission to print everything you told me today?

23. Is there anything you would *not* want me to print?

"Best wishes with your campaign."

Painfully True

We continue with Tom Moe's account of what transpired after he landed in the jungles of North Vietnam. Other stories follow. Much of this is very painful to read, but I would add this to the list that every American and every politician worldwide should experience. That list would include, *Schindler's List*, *Saving Private Ryan*, and *We Were Soldiers*.

Pure Torture
Thomas Nelson Moe

I was hiding under a log. Doing my best to masquerade as North Vietnam terrain, I'd pulled branches on top of me, smeared mud on my face, and arranged leaves and other foliage to stick out of my clothes. I was 20 miles behind enemy lines, having parachuted out of my F-4C fighter aircraft when a weapon malfunction blew it, along with my wingman, to bits. So far my terrain act was working; a group of North Vietnamese soldiers had passed, unaware of my presence, within six feet of me.

I'd heard on my survival radio that two other pilots had been rescued on the day of our mishap. Now, after three days in the cold and rainy jungle, I knew planes were on their way for me. It looked like a question of who would find me first.

I was eventually betrayed by a small hole in my camouflage through which I poked my radio antenna. Within seconds a zillion rifles were pointed straight at my head. Thus began a month-long, 100-mile journey to the "Hanoi Hilton" to begin my five years as a prisoner of war—

Within seconds a zillion rifles were pointed straight at my head.

where I would get to know pain on a personal basis.

North Vietnamese policy was that POWs were war criminals, a policy that supposedly justified brutal treatment and total control. That control was reflected by a list of regulations posted in each cell. Rule number one was the catchall: "Criminals will strictly follow all regulations or be severely punished."

The scenario was quite simple. An interrogator would tell you to do something, like give out military information. When, predictably, you would refuse, you were told you had violated the regulations and had to be punished. The word *punish* still evokes in me a slight feeling of nausea since it meant, at the very least, beatings that would last several days and nights. Punishment ultimately meant [torture], and to torture was to extract submissiveness. I found you could be tortured for accusing them of using torture.

147

Torture is methodically applied pain to produce a wearing effect—to make you submit. Usually the pain would reach a level just short of stopping vital functions, although it could continue even after one lost consciousness.

Its preliminary stages could start with something as simple as being sat on a stool, dressed in long pajamas (in summer) or just shorts (in the winter). The summer jungle air was suffocating; the damp, cold winter air was penetrating. After a while, you became a lump of huddled misery, sitting in the heat or biting cold. During a single session I sat on a stool in the same position 24 hours a day for 10 straight days. Sometimes the guards would tie you to the stool with your wrists strapped to your ankles, but usually you were left untied and told not to move, only being allowed to get up to visit the putrid waste bucket in the corner. And the guards were always nearby. If you moved a muscle, they'd pummel you with their fists and gun butts until they tired. I don't remember sleeping during these periods—just pain and the interminable passage of time.

After I spent days being worn down, interrogators would enter the scene, curiously almost a welcome break from "stool time." Tired and numb, many of us prisoners at first would give name, rank, and serial number—like you see in the movies. But this is fool's play and contrary to our military training, because this open belligerency would earn some pretty tough knocks. To survive you had to get your mind going and overcome the tendency to react with your emotions. You had to fight through the haze of fatigue to recall the specialized training, and it worked. Although the interrogations and torture rarely lightened up, with the resistance techniques we were taught we were able to avoid giving any useful or classified information.

I was fortunate because, as a young lieutenant fresh out of pilot training on my first assignment, I didn't know anything of real worth. The senior officers were really under the gun. If the enemy wanted something and knew you knew it, they would stop at nothing to get it. Thus we were trained to be clever, an actor under stress.

What I was not prepared for were the effects of solitary confinement. For the first nine months of my captivity, and sporadically later, I didn't see, hear or talk to another American. Although physical pain was inflicted on me deliberately and effectively, I would discover what an incredible burden mental pain would add to my suffering, how a dark fog slowly could creep over my consciousness, trying to rob me of my remaining power of reasoning. I saw that the mind could convince life itself to slip away through the beckoning black hole that pain created. I learned how vital it was to keep the mind as sharp as possible.

This was necessary to get through interrogations and also for survival. If you didn't keep your mind clear, the "V," as we called the North Vietnamese, would crush you through a steady dose of pain that eroded mind and body like a vicious chemical.

The body is first to give up. You cannot keep yourself from passing out, throwing up, screaming. I discovered that the more the body convulsed involuntarily, the more I could observe it as though it belonged to someone else. I found I could intellectualize pain, which allowed me to take a quantum leap in my tolerance of it. Sometimes, though, the problem was staying in touch with reality enough to keep alive. Detaching oneself too much has an insidious narcotic effect that invades one's reason and dulls normal danger signals. This is probably the way nature helps us die without being all tensed up.

I walked a psychic tightrope between too much pain and too much mental retreat from reality. That meant fighting back against the siren lure of pain-free death. Sometimes I knew I needed to feel pain. Pain could keep my senses sharp, my contact with reality stronger. I recalled the saying, "Pain purifies." This may not be entirely sensible, but it was curiously relevant then. Sometimes I would try to observe the pain process and translate the feeling into some sort of metaphysical experience—something interesting to contemplate, something detached. Sometimes when the pain got to be too much for the physical side of me, nature would take over and I would simply pass out.

I based my mental retreats not on fantasy but on real things. I designed and built homes, about ten of them—some dream houses, others more practical. First I made a floor plan, then the exterior, and then I would build them in my mind nail by nail, down to the most minute detail. I'd design it, lay the cement, put up the two-by-fours, drive each nail, and even saw each board—slowly. If it progressed too fast, I would envision a bad cut on a board and resaw it.

If I could help it, this was not going to be the place where I cashed it in.

I made lists. I made a list of every country I could think of, then every capital. I even made a list of all the candy bars I could think of. I tried to think of everything I had ever learned; once I reviewed everything I'd learned about trees. Sometimes I'd derive mathematical formulas, spending hours in the process. I could get completely wrapped up in this, completely escaping into my mind. With mental exercise came resolve—if I could help it, this was not going to be the place where I cashed it in.

A Relentless Search

Isolation lasted about nine months, until I was moved to another prisoner of war camp in Hanoi. There I got a roommate, Myron Donald from Moravia, New York. For more than a year we lived together in a windowless concrete bunker we called the Gunshed. During that time Myron would save my life.

It was a hot box, the Gunshed, so hot we could hardly breathe. It was so stifling that just to breathe we often lay by a small slit under the door through which our jailers slid food.

The food itself was used against us like everything else. It usually consisted of watery green soup (we called it weeds) and a chunk of tasteless bread. The soup was delivered boiling hot in the summer and stone cold in the winter. When it was hot we couldn't take a mouthful, since eating raises the body metabolism and thus body heat. If the guards didn't return too quickly, we would let the food sit until dark and the room temperature had slacked off to, maybe, 110 degrees.

We perspired so much our skin became waterlogged, looking like pale cheese, a crumbling coat of slimy flesh often festering with rash and fungus. Horribly dehydrated, we got only two little teapots of putrid water a day, and we used some of it to dampen our faces and wash off the crumbling skin. On top of this, mosquitoes were thick, their wings creating a constant chorus, and the room stank of the waste bucket. Rat droppings seasoned the food along with razor blades, glass, stones, and pieces of wire. Actually some of this unexpected booty came in handy.

After about a year of captivity when, oddly, I was getting accustomed to the harshness, my journey took me down an even darker path. The situation developed slowly. First I was told I might win an early release if I would cooperate and meet with some visiting delegations—anti-war groups or radical Hollywood personalities—and tell them I had been treated well. I refused these special favors and at any rate would not participate in their propaganda. When they kept pressuring me, I went on a hunger strike—an emaciated prisoner would not make good propaganda, I reasoned. This got me off the go-home-early list but angered my jailers, if only because I was not submissive. Thus began the really hard stuff.

Things started with long sessions of standing immobile around the clock; next I was put on my knees for three, four, six hours at a time. This went on for days. It was the first phase, sort of a limbering-up session to wear me out and take the edge off my powers of reasoning. Then I was told to write a war-crimes confession, saying I was sorry I'd participated in the war. When I refused, I got to serve as a stress reliever for about 20 guards—each took his turn beating me to a pulp. They pounded me for six or eight hours. By then I was getting pretty shaky. Then they got serious. I was introduced to a bowl of water, some filthy rags and a steel rod. The guards stuffed a rag in my mouth with the rod, then, after putting another rag over my face, they slowly poured the water on it until all I was breathing was water vapor. I could feel my lungs going tight with fluid and felt like I was drowning. I thrashed in panic as darkness took over. As I passed out, thinking I was dying. I remember thanking God that we had made a stand against this kind of society.

When my senses returned I discovered I had been blindfolded and trussed into the "pretzel" position. Thick leg irons shackled my ankles, my wrists were tied behind me, and a rope bound my elbows just above the joints. The guards tightened the bindings by putting their feet against my arms and pulling the ropes until they couldn't pull any harder. Then they tied my wrists to my ankles and jammed a 10-foot pole between my back and elbows. After a few hours the leg irons began to press heavily on my shins and feet like a vise. The ropes strangled my flesh, causing searing pain and making my arms go numb and slowly turn black.

In the middle of the night, one of the less hostile guards, whom we called Mark, sneaked in and loosened the ropes a little. If he hadn't, I'm sure I would have lost both arms. In this case I would have vanished with the other badly injured POWs who never were repatriated.

After a few hours, the guards came back and jerked up on the pole, lifting me up and down by my elbows, then slamming me to the floor on my face or backward on my head. This went on through the early morning hours.

At dawn two Vietnamese officers casually strolled in. I told them they might kill me, but I still wasn't interested in their propaganda. They laughed and calmly said, "It's easy to die but hard to live, and we'll show you just how hard it is to live."

Indeed the pain got to the point where I truly wanted to die. My mind games weren't sufficient to help me manage any more pain. I tried screaming to relieve the stress until the grimy rag was stuffed back into my mouth. I tried doing anything to take my mind away from what was happening, but I couldn't. My prayers became desperate gasps. The only solution was to stop living, but what can you do when you're tied up? You can't will your heart to stop beating.

After about a week I finally told the guards I'd write the confession. I had to get out of the ropes, collect my thoughts, and perhaps muster a bit more strength to still do nothing or at least moderate what would happen. My hosts knew exactly what I was thinking and simply said, "It's too late." They brought in a guard, who sported the only leather boots I ever saw in North Vietnam. I don't know what they told him, but he looked like he wanted to kill me. He looked insane, his eyes wide open, and he practically jumped up and down when they turned him loose on me.

From my point of view, what went on next didn't last long. He began by kicking me in the back with all the strength he could exert. After this first savage kick, just one kick, I knew I'd been badly injured, maybe mortally. The pain was grave, more of a deep sickening feeling. My mind floated free of my body as if I were a spectator, not a participant. I was beyond pain.

> **My mind floated free of my body as if I were a spectator, not a participant. I was beyond pain.**

Sometime the next day the guards untied me, and I sprawled on the bloody floor, red fluid oozed out of every opening in my body. I had no strength to sit or stand; I just sort of unrolled. In spite of my sorry state, I did not want to look undignified, so I tried to get up. I managed to crawl to a corner and sit leaning against the wall, trying desperately to gather my thoughts.

We spent the next three days working on the war-crimes confession, but the guards would wave whatever I wrote in my face and scream that it wasn't satisfactory. Were they seeing through my innuendos and double meanings? I could feel myself starting to panic as I could feel my last remaining defenses slipping.

The demands increased now to a taped confession. Somehow I still found the strength to refuse—perhaps a little bit too resolutely, because they reverted to the hard stuff again. I was having trouble remembering those precious resistance techniques I had been taught so many light-years ago. I started making a tape, pushing my sluggish brain to come up with ideas to show acceptable submissiveness to my wards yet useless for propaganda. My attempts were not convincing, so the torture continued. I told myself just to make it one more day, and then just one more. Anyone trained in such affairs knows that constant torture can make captives reach a point where they can't maintain mental equilibrium, and my captors knew it too. They could break me, and I was becoming frantic, fearing my strength would not last.

Then, they stopped—just like that. Some weeks had gone by, and perhaps they had other business. Maybe they figured I might not make it. Although they had murdered prisoners, I believe most of my colleagues who died were accidentally tortured to death. The North Vietnamese knew they could not win the war militarily, but they might succeed if they garnered world sympathy. It would be difficult for them to look good if too many POWs "died in captivity." But I came pretty close, as did many of my mates.

My immediate challenge was to recover from the kidney and chest injuries from that wild night of "kick the Yankee." My entire body was bloated, my eye sockets two puffy slits. You could stick your finger into me up to your knuckle and pull it out leaving a hole that would slowly fill with fluid. Myron didn't recognize me at first when I was thrown back into our cell. He set my broken ribs with his fingertips and used our shirts to bind my chest. Occasionally the ribs would click out of place, and he would reset them. But it didn't take long after I was on the mend for the torture sessions to resume.

As I grew more and more weary, I had to cope with one of the most corrosive elements of the human spirit—hate. Hate is a terrible distraction, a horribly destructive human enterprise. Hate invades the consciousness when the mind's reasoning power fades. Hate is a way we assign blame for our plight when our faith weakens and our resolve becomes clouded. Pain intensifies hate, making us want to strike out at something.

I stumbled into this blackness and, with vivid flashes of bitter invectives, cursed everything I had held sacred. I bathed in self-pity and resolved all my sufferings with the most wicked solutions. Although I drew some strength from hate, I finally realized I was drawing it from the devil. I journeyed into the lowest point in my life. And then I was truly exhausted.

I "came to" after a particularly horrific torture session, alone, lying on a stone floor, more naked than clothed, bruised, filthy, gaunt, and panting in little puppy breaths. I felt surprisingly free of pain and acutely aware of every inch of my surroundings. I knew I wasn't very healthy, and I was startled at how my body looked like a bag of left-over chicken bones.

My knees looked huge compared to the rest of my scrawny legs. Lying on my side, I could place a fist between my thighs and touch only air. But I didn't hurt anywhere. I thought maybe I was dead. I thought about many, many things as I lay there almost motionless for days. I prayed and prayed and prayed.

Finally the cell door peephole quietly opened, and an eyeball squinted into the darkness. Then it was gone. A few minutes later the heavy wooden door opened with a clanging of keys and sliding bolts. An enamel plate skittered across the floor and halted just short of my slowly blinking eyes. On it was a mound of raw salt crystals piled on top of some rice. "The salt is for beriberi," the voice said, and the door banged shut.

I thought for a moment: *Does he mean the salt will give me beriberi or prevent it?* I chuckled to myself. My feeble attempt at humor was an elixir. Even though I would spend several more years as a guest of

Uncle Ho, I knew I was over the hump. Humor, faith and mental focus would allow me to endure. I felt human, mentally whole and refreshed.

Maybe there is something to that old saying about pain purifying, but I would not prescribe the treatment.

Captured in North Vietnam in January 1968, Thomas Moe was released in 1973. Two years later he earned a master's degree from Notre Dame, where he eventually served as professor of aerospace studies and commander of the Air Force ROTC program. He retired from the U. S. Air Force in the fall of 1995.[3]

Getting Through the Hard Times

How do you survive the kind of ongoing torture and irrational punishment that Tom Moe did? Where do you find the strength to stay in the game, day after day? Tom explained it this way:

There were two things that helped me get through the hard times. One was an appraisal of the situation. If I moped and dwelled on some cloudy dreamy future, it would be depressing. So I lived each day as it came. I considered that my real life was being a prisoner, so I should make the best of it since it was at hand. I should not get tangled up with the future so that my present survival would not be jeopardized.

The second thing, after accomplishing the first, was to plan for the future and try to do something in the present to bring fruit in the future. For instance, I learned French and Russian so that I might use them in a future-planned career. My faith in God became very real, but it was not a dependency faith. God gave the strength if I had the guts to do something and believed in an ultimate truth. Moral law as well as physical laws are self-evident, I discovered, and if I followed my conscience, I felt I could do no more, and God's truth would do the rest. I feel that I developed a strong faith in my country, but I also matured in my understanding of governments.

The reason we have and need a democracy is that men are weak, not always motivated by the most honorable intents, and through due process we maintain a clean society from top to bottom. That is, a firm trust and confidence in my leaders but not a naive disillusionment should a bad apple show up anywhere in the system, because the electoral processes could take care of that.

My military "career" before I was shot down was rather brief. I had enlisted in the naval reserve when I was 17 but also entered college a few months later, right after bootcamp in Great Lakes Illinois. Following graduation from Capital University in Columbus, Ohio, I was commissioned into the regular air force. My wife, Chris, and I were married the following September, after which we moved to my first assignment. I entered pilot training at Craig Air Force Base in Selma, Alabama. I graduated and went on to F-4C training at Davis-Monthan AFB in Tucson, Arizona. While we were there our first child, Connie, was born. I was then assigned to the 366th wing at Danang Air Base, South Vietnam. I flew eighty combat missions.

On January 16, 1968, a 750-lb. GP bomb detonated near my aircraft forcing me to eject. I spent the next five years and two months as a POW in North Vietnam. Following repatriation in March 1973, I entered the University of Notre Dame to begin a master's program in government

> On January 16, 1968, a 750-lb. GP bomb detonated near my aircraft, forcing me to eject.

to include an area studies certificate in Soviet and East European studies. One of my classmates was Condoleezza Rice, who went on to the very heights in government service. My language and geography studies in undergraduate school and Hanoi bore fruit indeed.

God has blessed my family with longevity through these years. My parents were still living when I came home; my dad lived to see me fly the F-16, and my mom to help my wife, Chris, pin on my colonel's eagles. Chris and I were blessed with two more children after I returned, my sons Erik and Ryan, who are both raising their own families.

The spirit of Operation Homecoming, which marked our return to freedom in 1973 was the very soul of the American family. I do not feel that the glowing happiness bursting out from everyone I have met was really directed at me or any specific man. It was a total spirit of happiness and helpfulness and devotion, which is our very society. I felt as if I was a *part* of this incredible outpouring of emotion, not an *object* of it.

I pray that our government, a reflection of popular will, will continue to be guided by talented, brave men and women. I am forever thankful that a united society of hardworking, generous souls made possible our homecoming. My heart goes to every American whose loved ones did not return safely. God continue to bless us all![4]

I flew sixty missions over North Vietnam, five over South Vietnam, and twenty over Laos. Most missions in NVN were interdiction. Most in SVN were either close air support or Ranch Hand flights in the DMZ with our C123 brothers. In Laos I dropped mostly mines or sensors. For the latter we flew jointly with the navy or the spooks laying down smoke at fifty feet and 500 kts to provide them cover. These latter missions produced an interesting "white knuckle" tour of the rocks.

159

My squadron had F-4 Cs and Ds. I met my demise in a brand new D model, which had just arrived from the factory—its first operational flight. I was a backseat pilot (one of the last before they turned over that job to navigators whose training was better suited for the backseat role).

After I had been knocked down, I hid in the bushes and evaded the enemy for three days before rescue ops focused the enemy on my position. During the attempt to rescue me on day two, one of the sandies flew into the ground only a few hundred meters from me. I felt the ground shake when he went in. His name was Robert F. Wilke, USAF . . . I inquired about him as soon as I got to Clark after our release in '73.

21 August 1997
Subject: Attempted escapes in NVN (No. 14)

Dear MM,

Thanks for the notes on escapes. I sneaked away from the guards during two different nights that I was en route to Hanoi and both times ended up in a dash through darkened villages. The enemy soldiers were more scared than mad when they got me back since they were afraid that someone would find out about it.

They finally ended up keeping me in leg irons for the last part of my journey to Hanoi. Neither of these escapades lasted more than a few minutes since a six-foot gringo in black jammies just didn't blend with the locals, even at night. I don't think of these events as much of an escape story since my freedom was short-lived, but I do recall that my heart rate must have been about at a million beats per minute at the time.

The morning after my first attempt, a young man in an oxford-cloth striped shirt and slacks dropped by to see me. He must have been on Christmas break from Berkeley . . . he spoke in a casual accent-free English that made my jaw drop. It seems he was buddies of the guys who were guarding me (we had "rested" in that particular village for several weeks because I had feigned a back injury). He was a little nervous though and told me that he really wished I wouldn't "leave the guards" without permission. I always wondered who he was and where he got his education.

Cheers from sunny Columbus, Ohio!

Tom[5]

A Final Word

My admiration for Tom Moe and many others whose mettle was severely tested in POW camps knows no bounds. They *are* the spirit of America at its finest. The American eagle has never flown higher than in their astounding lives. And Old Glory surely smiles when she thinks of them and their sacrifice.

13 Laughing in the Face
of the Enemy

Hanoi, Vietnam
23 February 1968

Those pilots and soldiers who were captured and imprisoned as POWs in Vietnam delighted in frustrating the enemy, and they used various methods of doing so, such as the Hanoi Hilton Room 7's singing. It was a great way to pass the torturous times they faced and to keep their spirits and pride up day in and day out.

Lt. Myron L. Donald was one of those POWs. He had served as weapons systems operator in a Phantom fighter/bomber flown by Major Laird Guttersen on a mission they were assigned on February 23, 1968. While close to Hanoi, the aircraft was hit by a missile from a MiG 21. Donald and Guttersen crash-landed near Haiphong, and both were captured by the North Vietnamese. Both were released in March 1973 with other American POWs.

Donald and Guttersen received torture and deprivation in the hands of the Vietnamese, but neither lost his will to survive. Donald says that the POWs' sense of humor was one of the biggest things that kept them going. He remembers times when POWs were in their cells with irons on their hands and feet, but they were laughing so hard that tears ran down their cheeks. "This," he said about the Vietcong, "drove them crazy."

Since the Vietnam War ended, more than ten thousand reports relating to Americans missing, imprisoned, or unaccounted for in Southeast Asia have been received by the U.S. government. Many authorities, who have examined this mostly classified information, are convinced that hundreds of Americans are still held captive in Vietnam today. These reports are the source of serious distress to returned American prisoners, because they had a code that no one could honorably return home until *all* of the prisoners returned. Not only that code of honor, but the honor of our country, is at stake as long as even one man remains unjustly held.

> **N**ot only that code of honor, but the honor of our country, is at stake as long as even one man remains unjustly held.

MOMENT TO MOMENT

Donald, who was promoted to the rank of captain during his captivity, tells about the moment a pilot's world turned upside down:

One of the . . . most difficult things with which to cope occurs the moment you eject. One moment a world that is familiar to you—a warm, safe cockpit, seemingly insulated from outside danger, a radio to bring the sound of your friends to your immediate proximity, and a mind occupied with a job you've practiced a hundred times. Then suddenly an explosion! The red ball of fire from the missile hits your engine and a shout comes from somewhere, "You're on fire! Get out!"

As soon as you pull the handle, it is very windy and noisy followed by a sudden change to nearly complete silence as your parachute blossoms. A short, quick descent until you land in the middle of a group of small, dark, foreign people armed with rusty old squirrel guns and brandishing machetes. In a few moments you are standing in a rice paddy in your underwear facing an alien world and people whose language you cannot understand.

You spend a few hours in a primitive village before a Russian-built helicopter takes you to Hanoi where the government gets you in its hands and begins to tie you into all kinds of shapes approximating pretzels. The feeling of complete and utter fear and helplessness caused by the cold, hunger, and knowledge that if you fight back you will be beaten even worse, can cause a state of shock that can last for days, months, or perhaps even years.

My mind was so out of whack, and my room was so dark that when I received my two loaves of bread each day and saw the little dark particles in the bread, I thought they were caraway seeds. How nice of the Communists to do that for us! It wasn't until I was in a brighter room several weeks later that I could see the little legs and bodies of the bugs that I had wanted to believe were caraway seeds!

Another incident that happened soon after capture concerned my black pajamas. I had two pair. I wore one pair until they were very dirty and then changed and put the dirty one on the other empty bed in my room. I don't mind washing my own clothes, but it wasn't until several days later when the camp officer inspected my room and wanted to know why I hadn't washed my dirty clothes that I realized I had been waiting for the maid or the camp laundry to wash my clothes.

I think there is only one way to combat this type of shock, caused by ejection or a car accident or whatever. That is to have been here before. Either to have read about it or seen another person's reactions and then formed your own ideas, or to have daydreams about being in similar unpleasant situations and deciding how you would handle them. By having a ready-made plan of action and by knowing what types of reactions to expect, you can operate on your pre-thought-out plan until your mind begins to function properly again.[1]

9:00 p.m.
Ho Chi Minh Trail, Laos
9 November 1967

On November 9, 1967, Lt. Lance Peter Sijan and Lt. Col. John W. Armstrong were flying their F-4C Phantom fighter/bomber on a mission over Laos. While flying low over the Ho Chi Minh Trail at approximately 9 p.m. the aircraft was hit by a surface-to-air missile (SAM) and crashed (at least this was the official report). They went down near the famed Mu Gia Pass in the mountainous border region of Laos and Vietnam. It was not until nearly six years later that it was learned what happened to Sijan and Armstrong. They were classified Missing in Action (MIA).

Sijan evaded capture for nearly six weeks. During this time, he was seriously injured and suffered from shock and extreme weight loss due to lack of food. The extremely rugged terrain was sometimes almost impassable, but Sijan continued to try to reach friendly forces.

After being captured by North Vietnamese forces, Sijan was taken to a holding point for subsequent transfer to a POW camp. In his emaciated and crippled condition, he overpowered one of his guards and crawled into the jungle, only to be recaptured after several hours. He was then transferred to another prison camp where he was kept in solitary confinement and interrogated at length. During the interrogation he was severely tortured, yet did not reveal information to his captors.

Sijan lapsed into delirium and was placed in the care of another

American POW. During intermittent periods of consciousness, he never complained of his physical condition, and he kept talking about escaping. He was barely alive yet continued to fight.

During the period he was cared for, he also told the story of his shoot down and evasion to other Americans. After their release, his incredible story was told in *Into the Mouth of the Cat*,[2] an account written by Malcolm McConnell from stories brought back by returning American POWs.

Sijan related to fellow POWs that the aircraft had climbed to approximately 10,000 feet after being struck. Sijan bailed out, but was unable to see what happened to Col. Armstrong because of the darkness.

In 1977 a Pathet Lao [the Laotian equivalent of the Vietcong] defector, who claimed to have been a prison camp guard, stated he had been guarding several Americans. According to his report, one was named Armstrong. Only two Armstrongs are listed as MIA. There is little question that the other Armstrong died at the time of his crash. The Defense Intelligence Agency places no validity in this report.

Sijan was finally removed from the care of other POWs, and they were told he was being taken to a hospital. They never saw him again. His remains were returned on March 13, 1974.

In the early 1980s Lt. Col. James "Bo" Gritz conducted a number of missions into Laos attempting to obtain positive proof of live POWs there, or better, to secure the release of at least one POW. Although Gritz failed to free any POWs, he returned with a wealth of information on Americans. One thing Gritz recovered was a U. S. Air Force Academy ring for the class of 1965 inscribed "Lance Peter Sijan." The ring was returned to Sijan's family in Wisconsin.

Lance Sijan was captured by the North Vietnamese. It is theorized that since the Pathet Lao also operated throughout Laos, it is possible that Armstrong, if he was captured, was captured by the Pathet Lao.

Although the Pathet Lao stated publicly they held "tens of tens" of American POWs, the U.S. never negotiated their release because the U.S. did not officially recognize the Pathet Lao as a governmental entity. Consequently, nearly six hundred Americans lost in Laos disappeared. Not one American held by the Lao was ever released.

Lance P. Sijan graduated from the U.S. Air Force Academy in 1965. He was promoted to the rank of captain during his captivity and was awarded the Congressional Medal of Honor for his extraordinary heroism during his evasion and captivity. In part his citation read this way:

Captain Sijan's extraordinary heroism and intrepidity above and beyond the call of duty at the cost of his life are in keeping with the highest traditions of the U.S. Air Force and reflect great credit upon himself and the U.S. Armed Forces. Sijan became legendary in his escape attempts and endurance, even to his Vietnamese captors.

John W. Armstrong graduated from West Point in 1949. He was promoted to the rank of colonel during the period he was maintained missing in action. The U.S. believes that the Lao or the Vietnamese can account for him, alive or dead.

This note was written by Major Norman M. Turner, 80th Tactical Fighter Squadron:

This is a song concerning Lance Sijan and others. From my notes exactly as I wrote it thirty years ago. This is factually accurate as we believed it then, including the call sign. We assumed all were dead on detonation. I never put music to it.

Major Turner's song was written in Osan, South Korea, in 1970 as follows:

The Ballad of Baffle Zero-One

Chorus:
Two Phantom ships went thundering
    Into the rain and wind
Their call sign Baffle Zero-One
    Their crews were four young men
Armstrong and Sijan, Morgan, Hunnycutt
    And none has ever seen them again
It happened on a stormy night
    About two years ago
It was a strange occurrence
    I'll tell you all I know
It happened like I tell it
    If you'll fill my glass with rum
I'll tell you of the fate
    Of Baffle Zero-One

They took their ships into the North
    To strike the convoy force
And the bomb load that they carried
    Was of a different source
New fuses had been loaded
    Malfunctioned it was found
And the four of them were dead men
    From the time they left the ground

They started on their bomb run
    Above that barren road

Life on a Short Fuse

Three minutes out, said Milky
    You're clear to arm your load
Two sets of switches moved to Arm
    Two sets of relays hot
Three minutes from eternity
    But the young men knew it not

Ten seconds out said Milky
    Prepare for my countdown
Their thumbs were tensed on buttons
    Four miles above the ground
And the last thing they would ever hear
    That night so cold and black
Was a voice that counted backward
    And the final codeword, Hack

The bombs that were intended
    To fall upon the ground
Had detonated at release
    And filled the sky around
With torn and twisted pieces
    Blasted from the pair
And caused by lack of interest
    By the ones who sent them there

The ones who knew about such things
    Said, no it could not be
The fuses were all good they said
    Load more and you shall see

And three more ships were stricken
And more lives spent and gone
'Till they finally admitted
Was the fuses all along

And all the men and aircraft
Were called a combat loss
And no one had better say it's not
The word was quietly passed
And if they knew who wrote this song
They'd nail him to the cross
But someone should have, long ago
Told those who bear the loss[3]

Honor to Whom Honor

The following article is reprinted from the June 1977 issue of *Airman*. The articles of the Code of Conduct, which appear throughout are those memorized by Capt. Lance P. Sijan as a cadet. (They have since been modified to reflect the service of women in the armed forces.) Capt. Sijan was the first Air Force Academy graduate to receive the Medal of Honor.

"Sijan! My Name Is Lance Peter Sijan!"
by Lt. Col. Fred A. Meurer (USAF, Ret.)

The Code of Conduct

Article I

I am an American fighting man. I serve in the forces which guard my country and our way of life. I am prepared to give my life in their defense.

The colonel, recalling the tragic events of almost nine years earlier, had been talking for more than an hour about the heroic ordeal of Capt. Lance P. Sijan, his cellmate in North Vietnam. Reaching the point in his chronology when Sijan, calling out helplessly for his father, was taken away by his captors to die, Col. Bob Craner's voice broke ever so slightly and tears glistened in his eyes. He agreed to a recess in the interview.

Article II

I will never surrender of my own free will. If in command, I will never surrender my men while they still have the means to resist.

"Okay Mom, you can come back in now!" The voice, coming from a tape recorder that day in early November 1967, gave immense pleasure to Mr. and Mrs. Sylvester Sijan, just as it had so many times for more than 25 years. It was especially meaningful now, coming from Danang AB, Vietnam. Their son had done his Christmas shopping early and, separated by half a world, was having some mischievous fun with his family.

Sitting in the living room of the comfortable two-story house in Milwaukee, Mrs. Jane Sijan tenderly related the tale of her son's tape. Across the street, snow was crusted on the park that gently slopes into Lake Michigan. Flames danced in the fireplace as Sylvester Sijan busily prepared to show movies of Lance's graduation from the Air Force Academy in 1965.

Everywhere was memorabilia of Lance and his brother, Marc, younger by five years, and his sister, Janine, 13 years Lance's junior. An oil painting bathed in soft neon light on one wall showed Lance in his academy uniform, smiling out into the room.

Along the staircase hung dozens of photos of the Sijans—their children, relatives, and friends. Football pictures of Lance and Marc abounded, for football is a tradition with the Sijans. Lance's Bay View High School team won the city championship in 1959, the first time Bay View had turned the trick since 1936, when Lance's father played on the team.

Family heirlooms, souvenirs from faraway places, and trophies dominated mantels and shelves. The most significant showpiece, however, was enshrined in a glass case. Resplendent with its accompanying baby-blue ribbon dotted with tiny white stars was Capt. Lance Sijan's Medal of Honor. It had been awarded posthumously.

Jane Sijan —attractive and dark-haired, her Irish heritage smiling through—continued her story of the tape from Vietnam:

"Lance made us individually leave the room as he described the Christmas presents he had gotten for us. He'd say, 'Mom, leave the room,' and then he'd tell everybody what he had for me. Then he'd yell for me to come back in, and he'd send someone else out."

Those Christmas presents were not opened that year, nor for several years thereafter. On Nov. 9, 1967, Capt. Lance Sijan was shot down over North Vietnam. For years no one at home knew his fate. The box of Christmas presents was added to his personal effects, and not until his body was returned to Milwaukee some seven years later did his family sort through his belongings.

On March 4, 1976, President Gerald R. Ford awarded the Medal of Honor to Sijan for his "extraordinary heroism and intrepidity above and beyond the call of duty at the cost of his life. . . ."

Article III

If am I captured I will continue to resist by all means available. I will make every effort to escape and aid others to escape. I will accept neither parole nor special favors from the enemy.

Life on a Short Fuse

R & R in Bangkok, Thailand, had been nostalgic for Lance Sijan. He told his family in a tape from the country once known as Siam that his drama teacher at Bay View High School—where Sijan had been president of the Student Government Association and received the Gold Medal Award for outstanding leadership, achievement, and service—would have been impressed.

As a sophomore, according to his mother, Lance had competed against seniors for the lead singing role in the school production of *The King and I*, which was set in Siam. Competition raged for six weeks, consuming Lance's energy and concern.

"One day," said Jane, "he walked in and said, 'Well, I'd like to speak to the Queen Mother.' I knew he had the part."

There were 21 children in the cast, and Sijan needed one special little princess. He and Marc had always doted over their sister, Janine, even to the point of arguing who would feed her, as an infant, in the middle of the night. Lance asked Janine, then not quite 4 years old, to be his daughter in the play.

Occasionally, the family listens to a recording of the play, Lance's rich voice sing-talking the role of the Siamese king that Yul Brynner made famous.

Sijan flew his first post-R & R mission on Nov. 9, 1967, in the back seat of an F-4 piloted by Col. John W. Armstrong, commander of the 366th Tactical Fighter Squadron. On a bombing pass over North Vietnam near Laos, their aircraft was hit and exploded. Armstrong was never heard from again. Sijan, plummeting to the ground after a low-level bailout, suffered a skull fracture, a mangled right hand with three fingers bent backward to the wrist, and a compound fracture of his left leg, the bone protruding through the lacerated skin.

The ordeal of Lance Sijan—big, strong, tough, handsome, a football player at the Air Force Academy, remembered as a fierce competitor by those who knew him—had begun.

He would live in the North Vietnamese jungle with no food and little water for some 45 days. Virtually immobilized, he would propel himself backward on his elbows and buttocks toward what he hoped was freedom. He was alone. He would be joined later by two other Americans, and in short, fading-in-and-out periods of consciousness and lucidity, would tell them his story.

Now, however, there was hope for Lance Sijan. Aircraft circled and darted overhead, part of a gigantic search-and-rescue effort launched to recover him and Armstrong. Aerospace Rescue and Recovery Service histories state that 108 aircraft participated the first two days, and 14 more on the third when no additional contact was made with Sijan, known to those above as "AWOL 1."

He would live in the North Vietnamese jungle with no food and little water for some 45 days.

Contact had been made earlier, and the answer to the authenticating question, "Who is the greatest football team in the world?" came easily for the Wisconsin native. "The Green Bay Packers," Sijan replied. In continuing voice contacts, "the survivor was talking louder and faster," the history notes. "AWOL did not know what happened to the front-seater."

The rescue force, meanwhile, was taking "ground fire from all directions" and was "worried about all the [friendly] fire hitting the survivor." Finally, Jolly Green 15, an HH-3E helicopter, picked up a transmission from the ground: "I see you, I see you. Stay where you are. I'm coming to you!"

For 33 minutes, Jolly Green 15 hovered over the jungle, eyes aboard searching the dense foliage below for movement. Bullets began piercing the fuselage, a few at first and then more and more. Getting no more voice contact from the ground and under a withering hail of fire, Jolly Green 15 finally left the area.

Rescue efforts the next day and electronic surveillance in the days that followed turned up no more contacts, and the search for "AWOL" was called off.

One A-1E aircraft was shot down in the effort—the pilot was rescued—and several helicopter crewmen were wounded.

"If AWOL," said the report, "only had some kind of signaling device—mirror, flare, etc.—pick-up would have been successful. The rescue of this survivor was not in the hands of man."

Much later, a battered Lance Sijan was to ask his American cellmates, "What did I do wrong? Why didn't I get picked up?" He told them he had lost his survival kit.

On that November day, except for enemy forces all around, Sijan was alone again. Although desperately in need of food, water, and medical attention, he somehow evaded the enemy and capture as he painfully, day by day, dragged himself along the ground—toward, he hoped, freedom.

But it was not to be.

Former Capt. Guy Gruters, who was to be one of Sijan's cellmates later, told Airman: "He said he'd go for two or three days and nights—as long as he possibly could—and then he'd be exhausted and sleep. As soon as he'd wake up, he'd start again, always traveling east. You're talking 45 days now without food, and it was a max effort!"

Col. Bob Craner, the older cellmate in Hanoi, picked up the story: "When he couldn't drag himself anymore and said, 'This is the end,' he saw he was on a dirt road. He lay there for a day, maybe, until a truck came along and they picked him up."

Incredibly, after a month and a half of clawing, clutching, dragging, and hurting, Sijan was found three miles from where he had initially parachuted into the jungle.

Horribly emaciated and with the flesh of his buttocks worn to his hipbones, Lance Sijan still had some fight left.

"He said they took him to a place where they laid him on a mat and gave him some food," Craner related. "He said he waited until he felt he was getting a little stronger. When there was just one guard there, Captain Sijan beckoned him over. When the guy bent over to see what was the matter, Captain Sijan told me, 'I just let him have it—wham!'"

With the guard unconscious from a well-placed karate chop from a weakened left arm and hand, Sijan pulled himself back into the jungle. "He thought he was making it," Craner said, "but they found him after a couple of hours."

Once again Sijan had been robbed of precious freedom. Once again he was down, but—as other North Vietnamese were to learn—by no means out.

Article IV

If I become a prisoner of war, I will keep faith with my fellow prisoners. I will give no information or take part in any action which might be harmful to my comrades. If I am senior, I will take command. If not, I will obey the lawful orders of those appointed over me and will back them up in every way.

Sijan's obsession with freedom had manifested itself much earlier, and rather uniquely, at the Air Force Academy. His arts instructor, Col. Carlin J. Kielcheski, remembers him well.

"He had the crusty facade of a football player, yet he was very sensitive. I was particularly interested in those guys who broke the image of the typical artist."

Kielcheski still has the "Humanities 499" paper Sijan submitted with his two-foot wooden sculpture of a female dancer. Sijan wrote:

I feel that the female figure is one of nature's purest forms. I want this statue to represent the quest for freedom by the lack of any restraining devices or objects. The theme of my sculpture is just that—a quest for freedom, an escape from the complexities of the world around us.

Kielcheski chuckled. "Here was this bruiser of a football player coming up with these delicate kinds of things. He was not content to do what the other cadets did. He was very persistent and not satisfied with doing just any kind of job. He wanted to do it right and showed real tenacity to stick to a problem."

Others remember different aspects of Sijan's character. His roommate for three years, Mike Smith of Denver, said he was "probably the toughest guy mentally I've ever met."

Sijan was a substitute end on the football team, Smith said. Football, he thought, hindered his academics, and his concern over grades conversely affected his performance and chances for stardom on the gridiron.

"He had a lot of things going and tried to keep them all going. He came in from football practice dead tired. He'd sleep for an hour or two after dinner and then study until 1 or 2 in the morning. He knew he had to give up a lot to play football, but he had the determination to do it."

Sijan did give up football his senior year. But one thing he did not sacrifice for studies was the company of young women.

"They found him very attractive, and he had no trouble getting dates," said Smith. "He was a big, handsome guy with a good sense of humor."

Maj. Joe Kolek, who roomed with Sijan one semester, agreed. In fact, he said, "It was pretty neat now and then to get Lance's cast-offs."

Smith recalls they talked sometimes about the Code of Conduct that was to test Sijan's character so severely fewer than three years later.

"We found nothing wrong with the Code. We accepted the responsibility of action honorable to our country. It was strictly an extension of Lance's personality. When he accepted something, he accepted it. He did nothing halfway.

"It seemed," Smith said, "that there was always a reservoir of strength he got from his family."

Sylvester Sijan, whose character and physique bear a striking resemblance to a middle-aged Jack Dempsey, owns the Barrel Head Grille in Milwaukee. Built into an inside wall is a mock 4-feet-around beer barrel top, a splendid woodwork fashioned by the elder Sijan from an oak table. A wooden shingle on the polished oak bears the engraved inscription, "Tradition."

Sylvester Sijan's forefathers immigrated from Serbia, a separate country prior to World War I that later became part of Yugoslavia.

"Serbians have been noted for their heroic actions in circumstances where they were outnumbered," the elder Sijan said. "They were vicious fighters on a one-to-one or a one-to-fifty basis, so they have a history of instinct and drive."

He thinks a mixture of that tradition, his son's love for his home, and his competitive spirit spurred him through the painful odyssey in Vietnam.

"What made Lance do what he did? One thing, for sure. He always wanted to come home, no matter where he was. He was going to come home whether it was in pieces or as a hero.

"Lance's competitive nature kind of grew with him," said Sylvester Sijan. "A person never knows how competitive he really is until he comes up against the ultimate situation. He could have been less courageous; he could have retreated into the ranks of the North Vietnamese and said, 'Here I am, take care of me.' But he chose to go the other way. He probably never doubted that somehow, somewhere he'd get out."

Lance Sijan had wondered about his ultimate fate even before leaving for Vietnam, according to Mike Smith. In the Air Force at the time and stationed at Wright-Patterson AFB, Ohio, Smith enjoyed a visit from Sijan, who was on leave prior to going overseas.

He had a premonition that he might not return.

"I sensed a foreboding in him, and he and I dealt with the issue of not coming back," Smith said. "I remember it distinctly because I talked with my wife about our conversation. I felt he had a premonition that he might not return."

Jane Sijan, too, sensed something. In Milwaukee prior to leaving, Lance asked her to sew two extra pockets into his flight suit, and he took great pains coating matches with wax.

"One night he was sitting on his bed," she recalled. "He was sewing razor blades into his undershirts so he would have them if he was ever shot down."

Article V

When questioned, should I become a prisoner of war, I am required to give name, rank, service number, and date of birth. I will evade answering further questions to the utmost of my ability. I will make no oral or written statements disloyal to my country and its allies or harmful to their cause.

Capt. Lance Sijan had been on the ground for forty-one days when Col. Bob Craner and Capt. Guy Gruters took off from Phu Cat AB in their F-100 on Dec. 20, 1967.

Pinpointing targets in North Vietnam from the "Misty" forward air control jet fighter, they were hit by ground fire and ejected. Both were captured and brought to a holding point in Vinh, where they were thrust into bamboo cells and chained.

Reaching back into his memory, crowded with recollections of more than five years as a prisoner of war, Craner told the story:

"As best as I can recall, it was New Year's Day of 1968 when they brought this guy in at night. The Rodent [a prison guard] came into the guy's cell next to mine and began his interrogation. It was clearly audible.

"He was on this guy for military information, and the responses I heard indicated he was in very, very bad shape. His voice was very weak. It sounded to me as though he wasn't going to make it.

"The Rodent would say, 'Your arm, your arm, it is very bad. I am going to twist it unless you tell me.' The guy would say, 'I'm not going to tell you; it's against the Code.' Then he would start screaming. The Rodent was obviously twisting his mangled arm.

"The whole affair went on for an hour and a half, over and over again, and the guy just wouldn't give in. He'd say, 'Wait till I get better ... you're really going to get it.' He was giving the Rodent all kinds of lip, but no information.

"The Rodent kept laying into him. Finally I heard this guy rasp, 'Sijan! My name is Lance Peter Sijan!' That's all he told him."

Guy Gruters, also an Air Force Academy graduate, but a year senior to Sijan, was in a cell down the hall and did not know the identity of the third captive. He does recall that "The guy was apparently always trying to push his way out of the bamboo cell, and they'd beat him with a stick to get him back. We could hear the cracks."

After several days, when the North Vietnamese were ready to

transport the Americans to Hanoi, Gruters and Craner were taken to Sijan's cell to help him to the truck.

"When I got a look at the poor devil, I retched," said Craner. "He was so thin and every bone in his body was visible. Maybe 20 percent of his body wasn't open sores or open flesh. Both hipbones were exposed where the flesh had been worn away."

Gruters recalled that he looked like a little guy. But then when we picked him up, I remember commenting to Bob, 'This is one big sonofagun.'"

While they were moving him, Craner related, "Sijan looked up and said, 'You're Guy Gruters, aren't you?'"

Gruters asked him how he knew, and Sijan replied, "We were at the Academy together. Don't you know me? I'm Lance Sijan."

Guy went into shock. He said, "My God, Lance, that's not you!"

"I have never had my heart broken like that," said Gruters, who remembered Sijan as a 220-pound football player at the academy. "He had no muscle left and looked so helpless."

Craner said Sijan never gave up on the idea of escape in all the days they were together. "In fact, that was one of the first things he mentioned when we first went into his cell at Vinh: 'How the hell are we going to get out of here? Have you guys figured out how we're going to take care of these people? Do you think we can steal one of their guns?'

"He had to struggle to get each word out," Craner said. "It was very, very intense on his part that the only direction he was planning was escape. That's all that was on his mind. Even later, he kept dwelling on the fact that he'd made it once and he was going to make it again."

Craner remembers the Rodent coming up to them and, in a mocking voice, he paraphrased the Rodent's message: "Sijan a very difficult man. He struck a guard and injured him. He ran away from us. You must not let him do that anymore."

"I never questioned the fact that Lance would make it," said Gruters. "Now that he had help, I thought he'd come back. He had passed his low."

The grueling truck ride to Hanoi took several days. Sijan—"in and out of consciousness, lucid for 15 seconds sometimes and sometimes an hour, but garbled and incoherent a lot," according to Craner—told the story of his forty-five-day ordeal in the jungle while the trio were kept under a canvas cover during the day.

The truck ride over rough roads at night, with the Americans constantly bouncing eighteen inches up and down in the back, was torture itself. Craner and Gruters took turns struggling to keep an unsecured 55-gallon drum of gasoline from smashing them while the other cradled Sijan between his legs and cushioned his head against the stomach.

"I thought he had died at one point in the trip," said Craner. "I looked at Guy and said, 'He's dead.' Guy started massaging his face and neck trying to bring him around. Nothing. I sat there holding him for about two hours, and suddenly he just came around. I said, 'OK, buddy, my hat's off to you.'"

Finally reaching Hanoi, the three were put into a cell in "Little Vegas." Craner described the conditions: "It was dark, with open air, and there was a pool of water on the worn cement floor. It was the first time I suffered from the cold. I was chilled to the bone, always shivering and shaking. Guy and I started getting respiratory problems right away, and I couldn't imagine what it was doing to Lance. That, I think, accounts ultimately for the fact that he didn't make it."

"Lance was always as little of a hindrance to us as he could be," said Gruters. "He could have asked for help any one of a hundred thousand times, but he never asked for a . . . thing! There was no way Bob and I could feel sorry for ourselves."

Craner said a Vietnamese medic gave Sijan shots of yellow fluid, which he thought were antibiotics. The medic did nothing for his open sores and wounds, and when he looked at Sijan's mangled hand, "he just shook his head."

The medic later inserted an intravenous tube into Sijan's arm, but Sijan, fascinated with it in his subconscious haze, pulled it out several times. Thus, Craner and Gruters took turns staying awake with him at night.

"One night," the colonel said, "a guard opened the little plate on the door and looked in, and there was Lance beckoning to the guard. It was the same motion he told me he had made to the guy in the jungle, and I could just see what was going through the back reaches of his mind: 'If I can just get that guy close enough . . .'"

He remembers that Sijan once asked them to help him exercise so he could build up his strength for another escape attempt. "We got him propped up on his cot and waved his arms around a few times, and that satisfied him. Then he was exhausted."

At another point, Sijan became lucid enough to ask Craner, "How about going out and getting me a burger and French fries?"

But Sijan's injuries and now the respiratory problem sapped his strength. "First he could only whisper a word, and then it got down to blinking out letters with his eyes," said Gruters. "Finally he couldn't do that anymore, even a yes or no."

With tears glistening, Bob Craner remembered when it all came to an end. They had been in Hanoi about eight days.

"One night Lance started making strangling sounds, and we got him to sit up. Then, for the first time since we'd been together, his voice came through loud and clear. He said, 'Oh my God, it's over,' and then he started yelling for his father. He'd shout, 'Dad, Dad, where are you? Come here, I need you!'

"I knew he was sinking fast. I started beating on the walls, trying to call the guards, hoping they'd take him to a hospital. They came in and took him out. As best as I could figure it was January 21."

"He had never asked for his dad before," said Gruters, "and that was the first time he'd talked in four or five days. It was the first time I saw him display any emotion. It was absolutely his last strength.

"It was the last time we saw him."

A few days later, Craner met the camp commander in the courtyard while returning from a bathhouse and asked him where Sijan was.

"Sijan spend too long in the jungle," came the reply. "Sijan die."

Guy Gruters talked some more about Sijan: "He was a tremendously strong, tough, physical human being. I never heard Lance complain. If you had an

"If you had an army of Sijans, you'd have an incredible fighting force."

army of Sijans, you'd have an incredible fighting force."

Said Craner: "Lance never talked about pain. He'd yell out in pain sometimes, but he'd never dwell on it.

"Lance was so full of drive whenever he was lucid. There was never any question of, 'I hurt so much that I'd rather be dead.' It was always positive for him, pointed mainly toward escape but always toward the future."

Craner recommended Sijan for the Medal of Honor. Why?

"He survived a terrible ordeal, and he survived with the intent, sometime in the future, of picking up the fight. Finally he just succumbed.

"There is no way you can instill that kind of performance in an individual. I don't know how many we're turning out like Lance Sijan, but I can't believe there are very many."

Article VI

I will never forget that I am an American fighting man, responsible for my actions, and dedicated to the principles which made my country free. I will trust in my God and in the United States of America.

In Milwaukee, Sylvester Sijan started to bring up the point, and then he hesitated. He finally did, though, and then he talked about it unabashedly.

"I remember one day in January, about the same time that year, driving down the expressway; I was feeling despondent, and I began screaming as loud as I could, things like, 'Lance, where are you?' I may have murmured such things to myself before, but I never yelled as loud as I did that day."

He wonders if maybe—just maybe—it may have been at the same time Lance was calling for him in Hanoi.

"The realization that Lance's final thoughts were what they were makes me feel most humble, most penitent, and yet somehow profoundly honored," he said.

He still wears a POW bracelet with Lance's name on it. "I just can't take it off," he said, adding that "not too many people realize its significance anymore."

Though Lance was declared missing in action, and though one package they sent to him in Hanoi came back stamped " 'deceased'—which jarred me terribly," Jane Sijan said—the family never gave up hope.

"I'm such an optimist," she said. "I even watched all the prisoners get off the planes on television [in 1973] hoping there had been some mistake."

Lance's body, along with the headstone used to mark his grave in North Vietnam, was returned to the United States in 1974 for interment in Milwaukee (twenty-three other bodies were returned to the United

States at the same time). At a memorial service in Bay View High School, the family announced the Captain Lance Peter Sijan Memorial Scholarship Fund.

"It is a $500 scholarship presented yearly to a graduate male student best exemplifying Lance's example of the American boy," said Jane. "It will be a lifetime effort on our behalf and will be carried on by our children."

Lance Sijan, U.S. Air Force Academy Class of 1965, would be thirty-four years old now. He is the first academy graduate to be awarded the Medal of Honor. A dormitory at the academy was named Sijan Hall in his honor.

"The man represented something," Sylvester Sijan said of his son. "The old cliché that he was a hero and represented guts and determination is true. That's what he really represented. How much of that was really Lance? What he is, what he did, the facts are there.

"We'll never adjust to it," he said. "People say, 'It's been a long time ago and you should be OK now,' but it stays with you and well it should."

"Lance was always such a pleasure; he was an ideal son, but then all our children are a joy and blessing to us," said Jane Sijan. "It still hurts to talk about it, but I have certainly accepted it. I'm a very patient woman, and I wait for the day our family will all be together again, that's all."

On March 4, 1976, three other former prisoners of war, all living, also received Medals of Honor from President Ford. One of them was Air Force Col. George E. "Bud" Day [See his story, "All Day's Tomorrows," *Airman*, November 1976]. Col. Day later wrote to *Airman*:

"Lance was the epitome of dedication, right to death! When people ask about what kind of kids we should start with, the answer is straight, honest kids like him. They will not all stay that way—but . . . that's the minimum to start with."[4]

14 Pulling on the Thread
of Evidence

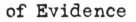

Bedford, Texas
February 2002

The more I researched, the more I found. So I kept digging deeper and deeper in hopes of pulling on the one thread of evidence that would cause the entire knotted issue to unravel. As I worked I kept my attorney friend, Jim Jameson, in the loop and bounced information and concepts off him. He helped by challenging me with ideas, leads, and legalities, such as in this e-mail from him:

> As I read your latest, I thought of Tom Clancy, who wrote *Hunt for Red October*. He was interviewed on C-Span a few days ago, and he said that he used no classified information in any of his books. That all the information was in libraries somewhere. He just had to dig it out. My thought was, If it is in a library, then perhaps it is on the Internet somewhere.
>
> Somehow, sometimes things transcend the normal, and there is no logical explanation. Somehow your cry for help may have reached Mr. Ratté. I'm sure that he will not talk to you, as he probably has a confidentiality agreement with Honeywell, but a mysterious voice

may inform you of someone who can talk. Also, somewhere in Defense, there is information about the altered fuses.

Someone signed off on that alteration. Ratté now brags about his accomplishments; therefore he at one time was proud of his engineering ability and idea. He may have patented his design or redesign. He may have written a book. If the plans and design of the atomic bomb are on the Internet, it would not surprise me if the design for the fuse for the bomb is also there.

One never knows. McNamara, if he is still alive, may know about the fuse. The Inspector General may know. Didn't you tell me that your wing commander went down because of a fuse prematurely igniting? Was there an investigation? Where are results of that investigation?

The most difficult thing about handling a products liability case is the investigation. What do you think would have happened if Ralph Nader had not written *Unsafe at Any Speed*? The fuel tank cases were difficult to prove. The Asbestos and Black Lung disease, and on and on, were difficult to prove. Once I had a Firestone multipiece truck rim case, and you would not believe how difficult it was to get the technical information out of Firestone. But we, many other lawyers and I, finally got the information. Usually a whistle blower is just waiting to go. If I remember correctly, the U.S. government must pay a whistle blower. Sometimes that is the incentive for giving information.

If I am not mistaken, Honeywell still has U. S. government contracts and is involved in bomb design. The object now, as I understand it, is to see how much punch can be put in a smaller and smaller space. We have gone so far since the bomb fuse matters that concern you, that it is most probable that that technology means nothing to anyone. I have never looked at the subject, but I understand that anyone who wants to can make a bomb. The only thing that the general public cannot do is get the nuclear materials.

In your spare time you might just want to learn how to make a bomb like the one that you delivered, and then you will be technically qualified to ask the right questions when the time comes. That is all that I can think of today. How fortuitous it was to have Mr. Ratté arise from the ashes. If you were Greek, you could thank the Fates.[1]

Jim later responded to one of my questions with the following:

As I said in my other note, I doubt if he will talk to you. My guess is that if John McCain called him, he might talk to him. At this point I would think about it for a few days and do as much "boning up" on the subject as you can do. He will more likely talk to you, if he believes that others have given some information. Once again, Honeywell is still in the bomb manufacturing business for the USA. You may be asking for a visit from the FBI, which wouldn't bother me, but you might not like it.

Honeywell is still in the bomb manufacturing business for the USA.

My off-the-cuff guess is that someone like McCain could ask someone else to talk to you, and that would prompt a response, such as someone near Defense who would love to expose another deficiency in the Vietnam situation.

In short, I would not contact Ratté directly now. Just think about it. Another thought: he is in a political campaign. I feel that he would not like to talk about his contribution to the death of many American fighting men.[2]

On February 19, 2002, I wrote this to Jim:

Further research showed that Phil Ratté has run for office thirteen times in the past twenty-six years. I can find nowhere that he ever won any of those races, probably because he runs on the Independence ticket in a state full of Republicans and Democrats.

My search for other info did not prove worthwhile. He doesn't have a book for sale on Amazon.com.

Jim responded this way:

No problem. Those incidents in captivity are hard to read. This is what the public should hear and know about when we contemplate war. There is more to dying than we ever could think about rationally. The people who carelessly care for the boys who are asked to fight and die need to have experienced a little of dying themselves before asking someone else to do it for them . . .

My source tells me to do a Google search on fuses, bomb fuses, bombs, and any other related subject matter.[3]

Bedford, Texas USA
20 February 2002

Throwing down the gauntlet, Jim went back to his law practice, and I went to work. After a few days, and eager to move this project forward, I wrote to Jim again:

I'm getting anxious to find out what we can learn from Mr. Ratté. How long before I can call him? I think it will be hard for anyone not familiar with our cause to do it for us and give us the results. I do think we have to be extremely cautious, but I don't think we can *not* contact him. Give it some more thought, please.

I have been known to "rush in where angels fear to tread," so I don't want to do that. How would you interview him?

Jim's response:

Here is what I predict: he will deny having anything to do with the fuse except that he was responsible for making it explode at ground level so there would no longer be any unexploded ordnance. He will claim that the fuse was perfect otherwise. He will know that *he*, not Honeywell, is responsible for any deaths caused by explosions near the delivering aircraft, because he altered the fuse from the design approved by Defense. So I would tread lightly and see where he wants to go, and let him lead. I do not think that a cross-examination will be fruitful. But you never can predict these folks who are proud of their work.

He will likely deny that he has ever heard of any bombs exploding at the time of drop. So really the question is where do you want to go with this, with him. There is a possibility that he will implicate Honeywell, so I would couch my questions toward Honeywell, i.e., tell him up front that all you want is information to bring closure to some of the families, and all you want to know is if Honeywell or someone else has knowledge about this type of explosion. Could he give you any leads as to where you can go for other information.

Since he is of the Independence Party, he may be a friend of the governor, who was a Seal, but I think that Ratté never served in the military. The governor might have some influence since he professes to be a great American.

I checked with ATLA, but did not find anything worthwhile, but I need to look again, as a Ratté has shown up in some depositions, but never as a witness.

You can always go back for a second series of questions, if he will permit it.

So, finally, just a conversational tone without accusations I think has the best chance of fruit. This type witness is always hard, because you do not have an opinion from him going into the questions.

So sail on and get what you can, knowing that he may be defensive. I guess now is as good as anytime. Preferably at his home via telephone, or send someone to meet with him personally, at home.

Good luck. Let me know what you learn.[4]

Phone Interview with Phil Ratte
25 February 2002

I spoke with Phil Ratté for more than forty minutes on the afternoon of February 25, 2002. Apparently my heuristic questions worked well, as he unloaded on me, usually ahead of the questions I had prepared. It seems that he has run for office thirteen times in the past twenty-six years and never won an election! He told me that forty-one people in Minnesota had run for offices on the Independence ticket and none had been elected, except the governor.

I learned early on that, although he had designed a nose bomb fuse, Honeywell did not accept it for production, at least not to his knowledge. Honeywell had a new electronic fuse that they were going to sell to the government for $130, instead of the $15 fuse Mr. Ratté designed. He went to a meeting, he said, with top-ranking military officials, and they were trying to solve the problem of bombs not exploding when they hit a hard surface like concrete. According to Mr. Ratté, thirty marines were killed by a bomb that bounced off a concrete bunker and exploded when it hit their position. He said the current bomb fuse then was a "lousy design." Phil explained that he had changed the design with people "on their lunch hours" making a fuse. To the utter amazement and surprise of his boss, Phil pulled his cheap fuse out of his briefcase during the meeting with the military, who wanted to know how soon they could have it in the field. His boss cut him off at that point.

Honeywell refused to consider Ratté's fuse, because they would make more money on the electronic fuse. Mr. Ratté was so disturbed by their decision, he packed his things, walked into the boss's office, and resigned, effective immediately. He gave me the name of his boss at Honeywell, stating that he believed he was still alive.

Apparently Honeywell, "through political connections," was a "sole source" for fuses. What really surprised me about Mr. Ratté was his adamant denial of any knowledge concerning the tail fuses. He only knew about nose fuses.

Honeywell was operating out of a facility that cost them one dollar per year, including machinery, according to Mr. Ratté.

Mr. Ratté disclaimed any knowledge of an FMU-35 fuse. Jimmy was right, Phil denied any knowledge of fuses causing bombs to go off under the aircraft.

Ratté left Honeywell early in 1967. We discussed cluster bomb units, and he was familiar with the bomblets, but not the term "CBU."

When I asked for names of the generals and colonels who attended the meeting, he could not remember any of them.

195

What followed next was unsolicited by me, but highly interesting. Mr. Ratté revealed his belief that, since we had broken the Japanese codes, our government knew about Pearl Harbor in advance. He then asked if I remembered the Payne Stewart tragedy. In that situation, when Stewart's plane did not turn on course over Atlanta, an air force plane was scrambled and flew close enough to see frost on the windows. "The air force plane reached Payne in nine and a half minutes." When the planes that hit the twin towers in New York and Washington, DC, left their courses, no planes were scrambled, and the controllers "knew it for more than thirty minutes."

Mr. Ratté next asked me if I believed "we really landed on the moon." I explained that I had known Astronaut James Irwin and fully believed he walked on the moon. Mr. Ratté agreed that "James was an honorable man," but he said he had "gotten to the point of not trusting the government on anything."

Phil and I joked about getting a visit from the FBI after all this bomb talk. He then told me he had, in fact, been visited by the Secret Service, and when they left, his copy of the "Magruder Film" (a film of the John F. Kennedy assassination) had been erased from a video tape he owned. He believed President Kennedy had been shot from the front, not the rear as the history books have it.

I asked Mr. Ratté if I had his permission to print anything he had told me, and he graciously granted my request. I also asked if I might call again, and he agreed with that. He said he would do some research on people that I might talk to about the fuses, and I could leave my name and number on his line, and he would call me. I tried to give him my number while there, but I guess he had nothing handy with which to write and wanted me to call back and leave a message.

Mr. Ratté indicated he was in the military for several years after leaving college, sometime from 1958 to 1962. He had worked for Honeywell during his last two years of college and went back there in 1965. He further stated that none of our conversation was "classified." He did admit to having plans and designs of fuses. I could not determine exactly why the Secret Service called on him.

Mr. Ratté referred me to the Picatinny Arsanal in New Jersey as the testing site for ordnance information. I attempted to find them on the Internet, but the search was fruitless. I was unable to find any reference pages. I was also unsuccessful in finding Mr. Fairchild, Mr. Ratté's boss at Honeywell.

All of the fuses Phil worked with were mechanical, not electronic. In other words, they were used on unguided bombs. I did find a lead on a fuse that could be added to the M117, 750-pound bombs, such as we carried, that could be guided from an outside-the-plane source. These new fuses were tested in 1967 at the Armament Development and Test Center at Eglin AFB near Panama City, Florida. In 1978 they became known as the Paveway Series. The guidance system was developed by Texas Instruments with "the intention of creating a cheap system for giving any of the MK-80 series and other tactically important free-fall bombs, most notably the 750-pound M117," a more accurate way of hitting the targets. Tom Moe's ill-fated two-ship formation was scheduled to be a ground-radar controlled drop. Due to difficulties with their signal transmitter, they ended up using TACAN to guide them to their target.

Having finally interviewed Phil Ratté, I was *infused* with information ... and even more questions without answers. The main question in my mind was, *Where shall I go from here?*

15 Justice or Mercy?

Bedford, Texas
October 2008

I have lost my enthusiasm for solving the mysteries surrounding the defective fuses. I have finished my search for the culprits, primarily because I now believe I know who they are. I have never been a "giant conspiracist" thinker, but I must admit to being closer to one on this issue. It is possible, it seems, that such a condition can exist without the participants' awareness or voluntary subscription—a case of the end being a consequence of the means, if not the justification. Or stated another way, the end explains the means.

We can't ignore another elephant in the room either. Where do our loyalties fit into this puzzle? Are we at odds with the dead versus the living? Do I not owe my fellow officers the same benefit of doubt that I give to myself? We all knew the fuses were defective. Several of those who knew went on to become generals, up to the four-star rank and everything in between. Was it just "survival"?

Conversely, we have fellow pilots who died because of those fuses. What about them? What about their families? How do we make certain that this story is a part of the archives? These thoughts anguish and languish today because we have stirred them up or because they will not go away. Should more have been done for the families of men killed by our own weapons in the air than was done for those who were killed on the ground by friendly fire?

Today I do not pray for justice; I pray for mercy.

Carolyn and I were discussing this on the way to the grocery. She reminded me of the huge errors General Patton made during WWII, and yet what a great military leader he was. (I only remember his arrogance.) General Patton was also a product of his times. And so were we! In 1968 we were not a litigious society. We did not think in terms of lawsuits and settlements, certainly not in the military. Even today I do not pray for justice; I pray for mercy.

Therefore, on behalf of all my guilty friends, all of those who could have pressed this issue but did not, I apologize and regret that none of us acted properly toward the men who died and their families. I do pledge to do my utmost to have this story recorded in the archives of the Vietnam War.

THE ECHO OF LIFE

A man and his son were walking in the forest. Suddenly the boy trips and feeling a sharp pain he screams, "Ahhhhh."

Surprised, he hears a voice coming from the mountain, "Ahhhhh!"

Filled with curiosity, he screams, "Who are you?"

But the only answer he receives is, "Who are you?"

This makes him angry, so he screams, "You are a coward!"

And the voice answers, "You are a coward!"

He looks at his father, asking, "Dad, what is going on?"

"Son," the man replies, "pay attention!"

Then he screams, "I admire you!"

The voice answers, "I admire you!"

The father shouts, "You are wonderful!"

And the voice answers, "You are wonderful!"

The boy is surprised, but he still can't understand what is going on.

Then the father explains, "People call this 'echo,' but truly it is 'life!' Life always gives you back what you give out! Life is a mirror of your actions. If you want more love, give more love! If you want more kindness, give more kindness! If you want understanding and respect, give understanding and respect! If you want people to be patient and respectful to you, give patience and respect! This rule of nature applies to every aspect of our lives." Life always gives you back what you give out. Your life is not a coincidence but a mirror of your own doings.[1]

AND NOW, DEAR READER, WE'RE COMING FOR YOU!

Did you think we forgot to include you? Obviously each one of us has a responsibility in the ongoing positive and negative events in the world. We hope you were able to share our experiences, and perhaps you might want to write your own. All of our lives mean something to others. As I wrote these stories, I remembered names and faces of so many others who have influenced my life.

Somewhere out there in America is a person who has in-depth knowledge of the Honeywell fuse story. If still alive, that person knows where this all went wrong and could, if challenged enough, answer Tom's question: why did it happen? Someone is still carrying a deep, dark secret, and it is, no doubt, a heavy load. They are asking the same kinds of questions we are:

- Do I really want to tell all those widows their husbands did not die from enemy fire for their country?
- Do I want to tell them how it could have been avoided, if only_____?

I think it is possibly a dilemma with no answer. It is, however, a form of regret, and I am sure, in my own mind, someone out there has plenty of that!

LIFE ON A SHORT FUSE

The adage says, "Old soldiers never die; they just fade away." And yet many of us who have lived our lives on the front lines don't want to simply fade away; we want to go out with a bang, just as many of our comrades did. So even though we have retired from the military, we have *not* retired from life. Even though we know that our lives are only on loan to us from above and that it's life on a short fuse, we continue to have significant, important missions to accomplish, whether in the air or on the ground. And we hope and pray that our lives reflect the spirit of America and glory of God accurately into the world.

We revel in old war stories that we share at reunions periodically, but we look forward with anticipation to the greatest reunion of all when the battle of life is over and we finally see the medals we've been awarded pinned proudly on the chest of God—Great Commander and Chief of the universe. Now *that* is what I call a grand reunion! And I hope you'll be there with us to celebrate.

The Reunion

Autumn leaves rustling, together to the appointed place,
the old warriors come.
Pilgrims, drifting across the sand they fought to preserve.

Justice or Mercy?

Where they meet is not important anymore.
They meet and that's enough for now.

Greetings echo across a lobby.

Hands reach out and arms draw buddies close.

Embraces, that as young men they were too uncomfortable to give,
too shy to accept so lovingly.

But deep within these Indian Summer days, they have reached a greater
understanding of life and love.

The shells holding their souls are weaker now, but hearts and minds grow
vigorous remembering.

On a table someone spreads old photographs, a test of recollection. And
friendly laughter echoes at shocks of hair gone gray or white, or merely gone.

The rugged, slender bodies lost forever. Yet they no longer need to prove
their strength.

Some are now sustained by one of the "medicine miracles" and even in this
fact they manage to find humor.

The women, all those who waited, all those who love them,
have watched the changes take place.

Now they observe and listen, and smile at each other;
as glad to be together as the men.

Talk turns to war and planes and foreign lands.

Stories are told and told again, reweaving the threadbare fabric of the past.

Amending one more time the banner of their youth.

Life on a Short Fuse

They hear the vibrations, feel the shudder of metal as engines whine and whirl, and planes come to life.

These birds with fractured wings can be seen beyond the mist of clouds,

and they are in the air again, chasing the wind, feeling the exhilaration of flight, close to the heavens.

Dead comrades, hearing their names spoken, wanting to share in this time, if only in spirit, move silently among them.

Their presence is felt and smiles appear beneath misty eyes.

Each in his own way, may wonder who will be absent another year.

The room grows quiet for a time.

Suddenly an ember flames to life. Another memory burns.

The talk may turn to other wars and other men or futility.

So this is how it goes. The past is so much present.

In their ceremonies, the allegiances, the speeches and the prayers, one cannot help but hear the deep eternal love of country they will forever share.

Finally, it is time to leave.

Much too soon to set aside this little piece of yesterday, but the past cannot be held too long for it is fragile.

They say, "Farewell . . . see you next year, God willing."

Each keeping a little of the others with him forever.[2]

Rachel Firth

Epilogue:
Author's Remorse

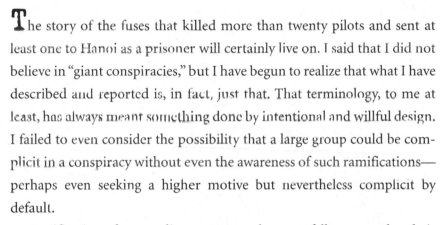

The story of the fuses that killed more than twenty pilots and sent at least one to Hanoi as a prisoner will certainly live on. I said that I did not believe in "giant conspiracies," but I have begun to realize that what I have described and reported is, in fact, just that. That terminology, to me at least, has always meant something done by intentional and willful design. I failed to even consider the possibility that a large group could be complicit in a conspiracy without even the awareness of such ramifications—perhaps even seeking a higher motive but nevertheless complicit by default.

Justification of our negligence to ourselves, our fallen comrades, their widows and children, and, yes, even the honor of our country were and are our defenses for our inactions and cover-up. Honeywell never intended to produce a defective fuse. Our military leaders certainly believed in our missions and the munitions to carry them out. The young ground crews, who unloaded the fuses from the ships in the harbor at Danang, knew nothing of their cargo. Those trained men who attached them to the very bombs which blew up under the planes did not know the words *complice*, *complicit*, and *complimented* lie next to each other in the dictionary. Our debriefing officers and their staffs were sworn to secrecy and had no roles in the decisions of weaponry used in combat. Our leaders in the chain of command (and who knows just how high that went) were victims of their own personal links in that chain. Our military schools stress that following the chain of command puts decision making at ever increasingly higher levels. As one officer waits for a higher level of decision, and no decision comes, matters such as this pass the stage of necessity.

Result? No-bill, no charges, no lawsuits, no lawyers, no judges, no juries, and no one punished except the lost comrades for whom I write.

To the dead I plead, "Cry out no longer!"

To the widows and their children, please forgive me if I caused you further pain.

To you, the readers, please close the chapters of your own lives and, as the apostle Paul writes, "Press on" to the higher callings of your lives.

And finally . . .

To Tom Moe

I do not know how to pay tribute to or honor you
for your sacrifice for our country
that would give you peace.
I can, however, dedicate this book to you,
and I do so humbly and hopefully.

Jack Livingston Drain

Notes

Introduction

1. Lynda Twyman Paffrath, *Angels Unknown* (San Mateo, CA: Lightbourne Books, 2002). www.angelsunknown.net. Used with permission.
2. Oliver North, *One More Mission* (New York: Harper, 1994).
3. Victor Davis Hanson, "The Meaning of Tet: 1968 Tet Offensive, Vietnam War," May 2001. www.victorhanson.com/articles/hanson050001.html. Used with permission.
4. Frank Snepp, *A Decent Interval: An Insider's Account of Saigon's Indecent End Told by the CIA's Chief Strategy Analyst in Vietnam* (Lawrence: University Press of Kansas, 2002).

Chapter 2

1. "Achy Breaky Heart," written by Don Von Tress © 1992 Universal Millhouse Music/BMI.
2. "Livin' on Love," written by Alan Jackson © 1998 Warner Chappell Music Inc/ASCAP.

Chapter 5

1. Tim LaHaye and Jerry B. Jenkins, Left Behind series (Grand Rapids: Tyndale House, 1996–2007).
2. *Jurassic Park*, written by Michael Crichton, directed by Steven Spielberg, © 1993 Universal Studios.

Chapter 6

1. "The Times They Are A-Changing," written by Bob Dylan © 1964 Columbia Music.
2. J. A. Engel, "The Face of Evil: Language and the Mobilization of American Democracy for War, from Jefferson to George W. Bush." Paper presented at the annual meeting of the International Studies Association, Town & Country Resort and Convention Center, San Diego, California. 2008-12-12 from http://www.allacademic.com/meta/p98188_index.html. (accessed 8 January 2009).

3. Dan Eggen, "Alleged Remarks on Islam Prompt an Ashcroft Reply," Washington Post 14 February 2002. www.washingtonpost.com/ac2/wp-dyn/A7548-2002Feb13?language=printer (accessed 8 January 2009).
4. John Stuart Mill (1806–1873). Public domain.
5. Norvel M.Young, *Living Lights, Shining Stars* (West Monroe, LA: Howard Publishing, 1997). Used by permission of author's estate.

Chapter 9
1. Lynda Twyman Paffrath, *Angels Unknown* (San Mateo, CA: Lightbourne Books, 2002). www.angelsunknown.net. Used with permission.
2. Bennett Cerf, *Bennett Cerf's The Laugh's On Me* (New York: Doubleday, 1959).

Chapter 11
1. Frederick C. Blesse, Major Gen. USAF Ret., *Check Six* (New York: Ivy Books, 1991). Used with permission.
2. Mike McGrath, "Mac's Facts No. 45 (Room 7, Hanoi Hilton)," updated 25 August 2008. Used with permission.
3. Lynda Twyman Paffrath, *Angels Unknown* (San Mateo, CA: Lightbourne Books, 2002). www.angelsunknown.net. Used with permission.
4. Blesse, *Check Six.*
5. Thomas L. Moe. Used with permission.
6 Email from Jim Jameson. Used with permission.
7. Ibid.

Chapter 12
1. Email from Linda Paffrath. 18 February 2002. Used with permission.
2. Daniel Lovering. "Laos Faces Decades of Unexploded Bombs," *Boston Globe*, 11 June 2000. Used with permission.
3. Thomas L. Moe. Used with permission.
4. Ibid.
5. Thomas L. Moe. "Attempted escapes in NMV (No. 14)." Email dated 21 August 1997. Used with permission.

Chapter 13
1. Myron Lee Donald, as quoted in *We Came Home* by Captain and Mrs. Frederic A.Wyatt, ed., Barbara Powers Wyatt (Toluca Lake, CA: P.O.W. Publications, 1977). Text reproduced with date and spelling errors as in original.
2. Malcolm McConnell, *Into the Mouth of the Cat: The Story of Lance Sijan, Hero of Vietnam* (New York: W.W. Norton, 2004).

3. Norman M. Turner, Lt. Col. USAF Ret., "The Ballad of Baffle Zero-One" written in Osan, Korea, in 1970. Lyrics reproduced as originally written without punctuation. Used with permission.
4. Fred A. Meurer, Lt. Col. USAF, Ret. "Sijan! My Name is Lane Peter Sijan!" Airman, June 1977. Used with permission.

Chapter 14
1. Email from Jim Jameson. Used with permission.
2. Ibid.
3. Ibid.
4. Ibid.

Chapter 15
1. "The Echo of Life," author unknown.
2. Rachel Firth, "Reunion," as recorded in Check Six (New York: Ivy Books, 1991). Used with permission.

Recommended Reading

The following list is provided for the reader who wants more information about Vietnam and issues mentioned in this book.

Burkett, B. G. & Glenna Whitley. "Stolen Valor: How the Vietnam Generation was Robbed of its Heroes and its History." Dallas: Verity Press, 1998.

Burnham, Gracia, with Dean Merrill. "In the Presence of My Enemies: A gripping account of the Kidnaping of American Missionaries and their year of terror in the Philippine jungle." www.tyndale.com, 2003.

Dorr, Robert P. & Chris Bishop. "Vietnam Air Warfare: The Story of the Aircraft, the Battles, and the Pilots who Fought." Edison, New Jersey: Chartwell Books, Inc., 1996.

Harrison, Marshall. "A Lonely Kind of War: Forward Air Controller, Vietnam." New York: Simon & Schuster, 1989.

Kelly, Michael. "The Three Walls Behind the Wall: The Myth of Vietnam Veteran Suicide." 2140 36th Street, Sacramento, CA 95817. Copyright © 1997. Revised August 18, 1998.

North, Oliver L. & David Roth. "One More Mission: Oliver North Returns to Vietnam." Grand Rapids, MI: Zondervan, 1993.

Paffrath, Linda Twyman. "Angels Unknown: A story of healing after Vietnam." www.AngelsUnknown.net. Copyright © 2002.

Snepp, Frank. "Decent Interval: An Insider's account of Saigon's Indecent End: Told by the CIA's Chief Strategy Analyst in Vietnam." New York: Random House, 1977.

Stevenson, William. "A Man Called Intrepid: The Secret War: The Authentic Account of the Most Significant Secret Diplomacy and Decisive Intelligence Operations of World War II." New York: Harcourt Brace Jovanavich, 1976.

Summers, Colonel Harry G., Jr. Interview with General Frederick C. Weyand, U. S. Army (retired).

Westmoreland, W. C., General (retired). "As I Saw It and Now See It: An Analysis of America's Unique Experience in Vietnam." A speech given in February 1989.

Wetterling, J. D. "Son of Thunder." www.jdwetterling.com, 1998.

Wilcox, Robert. "Wings of Fury": From Vietnam to the Gulf War—The Astonishing True Stories of America's Elite Fighter Pilots." New York: Simon & Schuster, 1996.